ANDREW MARVELL

*Essays on the tercentenary
of his death*

edited by
R. L. BRETT

Published for the UNIVERSITY OF HULL by the
OXFORD UNIVERSITY PRESS
1979

Oxford University Press, Walton Street, Oxford OX2 6DP

OXFORD LONDON GLASGOW
NEW YORK TORONTO MELBOURNE WELLINGTON
KUALA LUMPUR SINGAPORE JAKARTA HONG KONG TOKYO
DELHI BOMBAY CALCUTTA MADRAS KARACHI
IBADAN NAIROBI DAR ES SALAAM CAPE TOWN

© *The several contributors 1979*

British Library Cataloguing in Publication Data
Andrew Marvell.
 1. Marvell, Andrew – Criticism and interpretation
I. Brett, Raymond Laurence   II. University of Hull
821'.4   PR3546   78-41136

ISBN 0-19-713435-1

*Printed in Great Britain by
Cox & Wyman Ltd.
London, Fakenham and Reading*

FOREWORD

THE essays brought together here were given (in a modified or shortened version) as the Ferens Fine Art Lectures in the University of Hull in February, 1978, and the University is grateful to their authors for allowing them to be published in this volume. The lectures were a contribution to a programme of events arranged by the University and the City of Hull to commemorate the tercentenary of Andrew Marvell's death. Marvell was born at Winestead, near Hull, and as his contemporary, John Aubrey, wrote, 'His native town of Hull loved him so well that they elected him for their representative in Parliament'; indeed, he served as Member of Parliament for the city from 1659 until his death in 1678. It was fitting, therefore, that the University and City should join together on the occasion of the tercentenary. On 10 February 1978 at the request of the City Council a Civic Service was held at Holy Trinity Church (where the poet's father had been a lecturer) at which the preacher was the Rev. Professor James Atkinson of Sheffield University, and this was followed by a Civic Luncheon at the Guildhall, where a commemorative address was given by the Lord President of the Council, the Rt. Hon. Michael Foot, M.P. The text of this address is printed, by kind permission of Mr. Foot, in this volume. The City Council also organized an exhibition of Portraits of Marvell and his Contemporaries at the Ferens Art Gallery, which included items lent by the National Portrait Gallery, the Ashmolean Museum, Oxford, York City Art Gallery, Temple Newsam House, Leeds, and various private owners. While this book is in the press the University will also mount in the Brynmor Jones Library an exhibition of manuscripts and early editions of Marvell's work, including items on loan from the British Library, the Bodleian Library, Oxford, and Trinity College, Cambridge.

It is hoped that this book as well as making the lectures available to a larger public will be accepted as an expression of gratitude to those who organized and contributed to these events. These are too numerous to list in full, but mention at least should be made of Professor Garnet Rees, the chairman of the co-ordinating committee, Mr. J. Bradshaw, Director of the City Art Gallery and Museums, Mr. G. Oxley, City Archivist, Miss Brenda Moon, Deputy Librarian, University of Hull, and Mr. C. J. Rush, Assistant Registrar, University of Hull. To these especially the University and the City owe a debt of gratitude. Above all, of course, this volume is designed as a tribute to Andrew Marvell and in honour of his memory.

R. L. BRETT.

ANDREW MARVELL

UNIVERSITY OF HULL PUBLICATIONS

CONTENTS

Foreword   v

I.   ANDREW MARVELL: LIFE AND TIMES
     by JOHN KENYON, *G. F. Grant Professor of History,*
     University of Hull   1

II. NATURAL MAGIC AND POPULISM IN
     MARVELL'S POETRY
     by WILLIAM EMPSON, *Emeritus Professor of English,*
     University of Sheffield   36

III. THE SHOOTING OF THE BEARS: POETRY
     AND POLITICS IN ANDREW MARVELL
     by BARBARA EVERETT, *Senior Research Fellow,*
     Somerville College, University of Oxford   62

IV. MARVELL OUR CONTEMPORARY
     by MURIEL BRADBROOK, *lately Mistress of Girton College*
     and Professor of English, University of Cambridge   104

     Postscript. A Commemorative Address delivered in the
     Guildhall, Hull, on 10 February 1978, by the Lord
     President of the Council, the Rt. Hon.
     Michael Foot, M.P.   119

     Index   123

I

ANDREW MARVELL: LIFE AND TIMES

by JOHN KENYON

ANY honest biography of Andrew Marvell must open up with
the cautionary statement that we know very little about him. We
know hardly anything about his childhood and adolescence,
except a few dates. It is not even certain which school he
attended, and the only relic of a seven-year period at Cambridge
are two formal poems which could more accurately be termed
exercises in Latin and Greek. We really know even less about
the next ten years of his life, when he was in his twenties, and
what few scraps of information we have are contained in a letter
written in the next decade by a man who at this stage scarcely
knew him. His financial circumstances, then and throughout
his life, are mysterious. For the 1650s, when Marvell was in his
thirties, we have two or three letters which tell us next to
nothing about the writer, though from the important poems he
wrote during this period, the most productive of his career, it is
possible to deduce something about his political opinions. For
the 1660s and 1670s, when he was a Member of Parliament, we
have a comparatively large number of letters, but even those
written to relatives or friends tell us little about Marvell himself,
and his letters to Hull Corporation are little more than formal
newsletters. Again, some reasonable deductions can be made
from his prose and poetry about his political and religious
opinions in middle age, but he was not given to reminiscence,
and his later references to his life as a young man can be
numbered on the fingers of one hand. Apart from a few lines by
John Aubrey, we have no contemporary description of his
appearance, his personality or his life-style. It has proved
extremely difficult to establish whether he ever married or not,
and a certain ambiguity even surrounds his burial. In fact,
Marvell must be the least known of our major poets, and it is not
surprising that many scholars have rather overreached themselves in detecting hidden meanings in his work.

As I have said, any account of his early life must necessarily be skeletal. His father, also named Andrew Marvell, was born at Meldreth, between Royston and Cambridge, in 1586. The family can be traced back to 1279, and as late as 1872 there was still a house in Meldreth called 'The Marvells'.[1] He went up to Emmanuel College, Cambridge, where he took his M.A. in 1608, and he appears as 'minister' or 'curate' at Flamborough in 1610. In 1612 he married Anne Pease, almost certainly of the family of George Pease, then Master of the Woolstaple in Hull, though this cannot be established. Two years later, in 1614, he was presented to the living of Winestead in the Holderness, a valuable and unlooked-for promotion for a young man, which he may have owed to the Pease influence, or perhaps to the independent favour of the Hilyards, lords of the manor of Winestead. It is clear that he was an able and effective preacher, a quality never common among clergymen, and at the time much sought after.

It was a welcome promotion, too, for children were soon born to him in the Winestead rectory, which unfortunately was demolished long ago. The first, Anne, was born in 1615, followed by Mary in 1617, Elizabeth in 1618, and in 1621 Andrew, the looked-for heir. (A second son, John, was born in 1623 and died a year later.) But in 1624 their father received another promotion, this time to be Master of God's House in Hull (the almshouse founded by the de la Poles, commonly called the Charterhouse now), and lecturer at Holy Trinity Church. So young Andrew Marvell grew up in the Master's residence attached to God's House. This was outside the town walls; in fact it was in the present position of the surviving Charterhouse, near North Bridge, set amongst gardens then and looking across the river Hull to open country. (This is clearly set out in Hollar's map of Hull in 1640.) So, although as a boy Marvell would obviously have been familiar enough with the bustling, congested merchant city of Kingston-upon-Hull, confined in a rectangle defined by the two rivers, the present Humber Dock Street and the southern edge of Queen's Dock Gardens, he would also have known the countryside quite well.

But Hull was rather more than a port. It was a major fortress and arsenal with a permanent military garrison, the pivot upon which the defence of the north of England hinged. To the west and north it was protected by formidable walls (recollected in the name of the street, 'North Walls' on the southern edge of the Technical College), and on the other side of the river Hull by a large fort, whose memory is perpetuated in 'Tower Street' and 'Citadel Street', and the name of this whole district, which is 'Garrison Side'. Even if he took no part in the Civil Wars—and this, as we shall see, is conjectural—young Marvell must have been familiar with military drills and exercises, and he put this to use in his later poetry, for instance, in these lines from 'Upon Appleton House':

> Well shot ye Firemen! Oh how sweet,
> And round your equal Fires do meet;
> Whose shrill report no Ear can tell,
> But Ecchoes to the Eye and smell;[2]

and in a letter to Hull Corporation in 1660 he recollected as a boy watching the town militia drilling.[3]

Meanwhile, he was almost certainly educated at Hull Grammar School, though we have no proof of this. As the historian of the grammar school says, 'Marvell's connexion with the school is as probable and as unprovable as Shakespeare's with that of Stratford-on-Avon.'[4] John Lawson also disposes of the hoary old myth that Marvell's father was headmaster of the school; in fact he would have been taught by James Burney up to 1632, when he left to be vicar of Beverley, then by Anthony Stevenson for just a year.[5] It may be significant that when he went up to Cambridge in 1633 he ignored his father's college of Emmanuel and took a sizarship at Trinity, Burney's old college.

One thing is clear, Marvell had an unusual command of foreign languages; he may have owed this to Burney, who was a formidable teacher, and no doubt his father helped. It is easy to assume that seventeenth-century grammar schools gave their pupils considerable fluency in the dead languages. Not so. 'Grammar' meant what 'grammar' said: a command of basic rules, the ability to translate a few useful tags and perhaps cobble together a family motto. Marvell had the quite unusual ability to compose Latin verse as easily as English, with complete command of the idiom. He demonstrates this in his 'Letter to Doctor Ingelo' in 1655, a long letter in Latin verse which he despatched to a friend who was secretary to Bulstrode Whitelocke, envoy at Stockholm.[6] John Aubrey says, 'For

Latin verses there was no man could come into competition
with him', and John Milton, himself one of the best Latin
versifiers of the age, testified to his skill. In the course of his
travels in the 1640s he also learned Dutch, French, Italian, and
Spanish.[7]

It is also clear that Marvell came to manhood a Puritan. But it
is important to understand the limitations of this term. Since
the Reformation there had been a tension in the Church of
England between those who regarded it as a hierarchic church,
dispensing a formulaic salvation to its unquestioning members,
and those who regarded it as a loose aggregation of believers
who were assisted by the clergy in their interpretation of scripture, but must seek their own salvation. There can be no doubt
that the elder Marvell was a 'Puritan' in this sense. He gradu-
ated at Emmanuel at a time when it was still one of the most
Puritan-orientated Cambridge colleges, and his lectureship at
Holy Trinity was precisely the kind of specialist post created in
many towns to enable a man to preach without cure of souls,
and therefore without having to deal very much with the con-
troversial Book of Common Prayer. Marvell later described his
father as 'a Conformist to the established Rites of the Church of
England, though I confess none of the most over-running or
eager in them'.[8]

A balanced state of tension was disturbed in the 1630s by
Archbishop Laud, who tried to swing the Church back to a
more conventional (his enemies said popish) position, playing
down the sermon, emphasizing communion, and in general
stressing the ceremonial aspect of worship. However, though
general histories of England, rightly or wrongly, tell us of a
violent clash between Anglicanism and Puritanism in the 1630s,
local histories are full of clergymen who followed their own
course of action without any particular difficulty, and so it was
in Hull. The elder Marvell was helped by the fact that by a
historical anomaly Holy Trinity was merely a chapel-at-ease
attached to All Saints', Hessle,[9] and the vicar of Hessle, Richard
Perrott, obeyed the orders of the Archbishop Neile of York to
beautify Holy Trinity in the Laudian manner in 1633. In 1639
Marvell appeared before the Archbishop's court at York and
was ordered to use more of the Book of Common Prayer with his
weekly sermon,[10] but this was nothing more than a reprimand,

[handwritten margin note: M's father Puritan but not most zealous]

and there is no doubt that what he was doing, or not doing, met with the approval of his congregation. He secured great prestige, if prestige he needed, by continuing to minister to them during a severe outbreak of bubonic plague in 1636 and 1637, and on his death they chose as his successor William Styles, a much more committed Puritan, who so declared himself during the Civil Wars.

No doubt his son imbibed much of his teaching. In old age the younger Marvell defined in peerless terms the attitude of a Puritan towards life and revelation:

Every man is bound to work out his own salvation with fear and trembling, and therefore to use all helps possible for his best satisfaction; hearing, comforting, reading, praying for the assistance of God's spirit. But when he hath done this he is his own expositor, his own both minister and people, bishop and diocese, his own Council, and his conscience excusing or condemning him, accordingly he escapes or incurs his own internal anathema.[11]

The words he used of Cromwell in 1658, 'He first put Armes into *Religions* hand'—and his whole attitude to Cromwell—imply retrospective approval of the Civil War.[12] However, this does not imply that Marvell or his father felt themselves persecuted during the 1630s, nor does it imply any particular attitude towards the civil war then approaching. Many men who became royalists had a Puritan attitude towards the Church and a considerable dislike of Laudian innovations—the famous Edward Hyde was one of them. In 1636, as a Cambridge undergraduate, Marvell composed some fawning verses in Latin and Greek in honour of King Charles, and he made many royalist friends; the poems he wrote these friends have caused many literary critics unnecessary perturbation. What was approaching in these years was simply a power struggle, but no one clearly foresaw it. After a series of quarrels in the 1620s over taxation and war, Charles I and his parliaments reached the point of no return. He summoned no more Parliaments after March 1629, but his attempt to impose Anglicanism on the Scots in 1638 provoked a national revolt, and in 1639 and 1640, with Marvell still presumably at Cambridge, large armies were raised, based on York but provisioned from Hull, to invade Scotland. The King failed to subdue the Scots and in November 1640 he had to call the Long Parliament;

in the meanwhile the munitions assembled for the Scots cam-
paigns remained in the citadel at Hull, and were later a source of
great interest to both sides.

In the meanwhile Marvell's father was embedding himself in
the merchant community of Hull. In 1633 his eldest daughter
Anne married James Blaydes, J.P., of Sutton, a member of one
of Hull's wealthiest families. Her children intermarried with
the Thompsons, who were already connected with her mother,
and the Blaydes-Thompsons persisted into the nineteenth century; one of them was Town Clerk of Hull from 1837 to 1858.[13]
The second daughter, Mary, was married in 1636 to Edmund
Popple, another prominent Hull merchant, who was sheriff of
Hull in 1638. Her son, William Popple, was always very close to
his uncle. Marvell's mother died in 1638, when he was seven-
teen, but his father married again within six months, to a widow
called Lucy Harris, who had been born an Alured. The Alureds
were a family of merchants-cum-gentlemen, perhaps the most
eminent in the district, who lived in the Charterhouse, the
converted Carthusian priory which then lay just to the north of
God's House. Young Marvell therefore probably knew his
stepmother beforehand, but in any case there is no reason to
suppose that his mother's death and his father's remarriage
caused him any unusual perturbation; the high death-rate made
such events a commonplace in the seventeenth century. In any
case, by the time of his mother's death he was far advanced in
his studies; in April 1638 he was elected a scholar of Trinity,
and in the summer he took his B.A. He then stayed on to work
for an M.A., which he would have taken in 1632. None of his
biographers make the point, but it must be assumed that he was
destined for the Church; he would not have stayed on at Cambridge for a sixth and seventh year otherwise. Indeed, it was the
obvious career for the son of a clergyman without private
means; he may well have expected to succeed his father in due
course.

But on 23 January 1641 his world fell apart. A boat taking his
father across the Humber to Barton was 'sand-warped' in a
squall, and everyone aboard was drowned. His body was never
recovered, and, like his son, he has no memorial in Holy Trinity. Young Marvell seems to have left Cambridge at once,
though his defection was not formally noted by the college until

September, and from then until 1651, ten years later, his doings are obscure.

Obviously he abandoned any idea of a clerical career, though he only had another academic year to go to his M.A. Perhaps he found the prospect uncongenial, something only taken up out of deference to his father, whose death had now released him. But it is equally possible, and in my opinion more probable, that he was simply penniless.

Marvell's finances have always been obscure, but his eighteenth- and nineteenth-century biographers, who airily suggested that he was 'in easy circumstances', that he had a modest but adequate private income, had no authority whatsoever for saying this; nor could they explain why in his thirties he was still working at the menial job of private tutor, and touting assiduously for a £200 a year clerkship in the civil service. These biographers in fact created the myth—Grosart tactfully calls it 'a floating tradition'—that he was subsidized by a wealthy Mrs. Skinner, whose daughter was drowned with his father in 1641; she was even supposed to have bequeathed him her fortune. Unfortunately, both these ladies have been blown to rags by the big guns of modern scholarship, and the money with them.[14]

In fact, Marvell's inheritance must have been slender, and it may even have put him in debt. His father probably enjoyed a good salary by the standards prevailing in the Church at that time, though those standards were not high, but there was never any suggestion of landed wealth behind him; why otherwise should he have left Meldreth? He had married his daughters well, but each of them would have had to have her dowry, and this must have deeply eroded any savings he had; the last of them, Elizabeth, married Richard More in 1638. In fact, there must be a strong suspicion that he remarried so promptly after his wife's death, and chose a woman twice-widowed, so that he could use her dowry to marry off Elizabeth. This was a common enough manoeuvre at the time, and tolerably safe provided the husband lived to a ripe old age. But Marvell senior did not, and on his death his widow was entitled to a jointure, a life income in return for her dowry (which she would in turn have provided out of the jointure left her by her previous husband). Lucy Marvell came from a wealthy family, of course, but by the prevailing conventions they would only help her in the last resort, and here the problem was exacerbated by the fact that her late husband did not even have a house of his own to bequeath her. Whichever way we look at this problem, and it is a common one in this period, the conclusion is that young Marvell must have been in a state of acute financial embarrassment in the 1640s, and perhaps for a good time after. (Unfortunately we do not know when Lucy Marvell died, or even how old she was in 1641.)

As a result young Andrew Marvell had to earn his living as best he could. There was a strong tradition in nineteenth-century Hull that he served a clerkship in a Hull merchant house, and when the building in which he is supposed to have worked was pulled down in 1829 mementoes were made from timbers; a wooden box of this nature was exhibited at Hull Museum in 1921. Some Marvell scholars are prepared to accept this legend as embodying a degree of truth, and so am I. Marvell's connections with the Hull merchant community made it very natural that he should try such a career.[15] In later life he maintained close contacts with his Popple and Thompson in-laws, all of them merchants.

But precisely when he served his clerkship (if he did) we do not know; and though it is fairly certain that he spent four years in the 1640s travelling Europe, it is difficult to be sure which years. After his father's death in 1641 the first definite information we have on him is in 1651, when he went to Lord Fairfax's house at Nunappleton. However, Hull was certainly not a restful place to be in the early 1640s. In January 1642 Charles I finally quarrelled with Parliament and left London; in March he retreated to York. He had already ordered Sir John Hotham to secure Hull, but when he appeared before the town on 23 April 1641, at Beverley Gate, at the end of the street called Whitefriargate, between R. S. Boulton Ltd. (Wholesale Tobacconists) and Burton's (Tailors of Taste), he was repulsed. He was repulsed again on 17 July, when he made a formal attack.

For the next eighteen months Hull remained outside the main theatre of war, though it continued to act as a supply base for the parliamentary forces in the West Riding under Lord Fairfax and his son, Sir Thomas. Meanwhile, Sir John

Hotham, the hero of 1642, lost his enthusiasm for Parliament, and in June 1643 he and his son, Captain John Hotham, were arrested and sent to London. The following January they were tried for treason, found guilty, and executed. Meanwhile in July 1643 the Fairfaxes were heavily defeated at Adwalton Moor, and Sir Thomas retreated on Hull. After a foray into Lincolnshire, the royalist commander, the Marquess of Newcastle, laid siege to the town on 2 September. Resistance was fierce, and the royalists could not stop the import of supplies from the river. The Eastern Association also sent reinforcements across the Humber under Colonel Oliver Cromwell, and on 10 October Newcastle raised the siege. In the fighting Marvell's old home at God's House was totally destroyed.

Marvell could have served his clerkship during these years, and he could even have taken part in the fighting; but if he had we would expect to find more traces of it in his later poetry, and we would also expect Milton to have mentioned it as a point in his favour when he recommended him for employment under the Republic in 1653. It seems more likely that he spent the war years abroad, returning to Hull in 1648 or 1649 before going to Nunappleton in 1651.

Milton's letter of 21 February 1653 to Bradshaw, the President of the Council of State,[16] is the main authority for Marvell's tour of Holland, France, Italy, and Spain in the 1640s, and its duration (four years). I do not think this last point need be taken too seriously. His poem 'Richard Flecknoe' places him in Rome in Lent 1645 or 1646; probably 1646, because he also ran into Lord Francis Villiers at Rome in December 1645.[17] His return to England can be tentatively fixed by his elegy for young Villiers, who was killed in the Second Civil War in July 1648.[18] He wrote a similar poem for Lord Henry Hastings, heir to the earldom of Huntingdon, who died the following year of natural causes, and a prefatory poem for Richard Lovelace's *Lucasta*, also in 1649.[19] Lovelace, Villiers, and Hastings were all royalists—indeed, Villiers was the younger son of the Duke of Buckingham, Charles I's evil genius—and a great deal of scholarly juice has been expended on this fact. But this takes no account of personal friendship, nor of the profit motive; turning out polished funerary verses at twenty guineas a time was one way for an impoverished poet to keep alive. It would be more pertinent for scholars to inquire why Marvell went to Spain, which attracted few contemporary English travellers; it was the traditional enemy, it had a foul climate, bad roads, and worse inns, and there was always the danger of the Inquisition.[20]

There may, however, have been a closer connection between Marvell and the Hastings family. Once the myth, created by his early biographers, that Marvell was in easy circumstances, was disposed of, it became obvious that he could not have afforded to go to Europe except as a private tutor, and in the early 1640s there would have been no lack of such posts; with the universities closed many more noblemen and gentlemen were sending their sons abroad to be 'finished'. Margoliouth suggested that Marvell's pupil was young Edward Skinner, of Thornton Court in Lincolnshire, which would have had the additional advantage of explaining the Mrs. Skinner myth.[21] This is perfectly likely, but it can neither be proved nor disproved, and the same applies to the Hastings connection. True, Marvell's poem on Lord Hastings does not demonstrate a very close relationship, and other contributors to this volume, entitled *Lachrymae Musarum*, included Dryden, Herrick, and Sir John Denham; but it is difficult to draw any conclusions from the lapidary formality of this kind of poem, and line 40 suggests that he knew personally Lord Hastings' mother, Lucy, daughter of Sir John Davies, who was no mean poet himself, and the author of a very well-thought-of history of Ireland.

However, we are back on firm ground in 1651, when Marvell entered the service of Lord Fairfax. In the intervening years, while he had been abroad, and perhaps later in Hull, events had boiled up to crisis after crisis. In the winter of 1644–5 Fairfax had been appointed commander of a new army raised by Parliament, with Oliver Cromwell as second-in-command. This New Model Army had defeated the King in 1645, and brought the Civil War to an end in 1646. King Charles had provoked the second Civil War in 1648, and had again been defeated by the New Model. Then Fairfax and Cromwell had come to the parting of the ways. Cromwell and his son-in-law Henry Ireton bowed to the opinion of the army and put Charles on trial. He was duly executed in January 1649. Fairfax stayed

away from the trial, and his wife made some famous inter-
jections from the gallery. Such was his prestige that he retained
overall command of the army in 1649, while Cromwell was in
Ireland, but in June 1650 he resigned rather than undertake the
invasion of Scotland. It was soon after this that he engaged
Marvell to teach his daughter and sole heiress, Mary, foreign
languages, and Marvell took up residence at the family seat of
Nunappleton, where he remained until 1653 or 1654. Here we
must assume that he wrote some of his most famous poetry,
including 'Upon Appleton House, to my Lord Fairfax' and 'To
his Coy Mistress'—though it would be unwise to associate this
with Mary Fairfax, who was only thirteen in 1651.

'Upon Appleton House', which is Marvell's longest non-
satirical poem, has been made to bear a crushing load of commentary and exegesis.[22] All I would say is, that this, and similar
poems addressed to Fairfax or about him ('Upon the Hill and
Grove at Bilbrough', and the Latin ode, 'Bilboreum: Farfacio'),
show the grip which the retired general exercised on his imagination, particularly in this stanza, in which he sets out Fairfax's
doubts about the use of force:

> What should he do? He would respect
> Religion, but not Right neglect:
> For first Religion taught him Right,
> And dazled not, but clear'd his sight.
> Sometimes resolv'd his Sword he draws,
> But reverenceth then the Laws:
> For Justice still that Courage led;
> First from a Judge, then Souldier bred.[23]

Black Tom Fairfax, though a shadowy figure to post:rity,
was one of the most revered men of his age, trusted by both
sides, and trusted for just the qualities which Marvell saw and
admired in him; courage and decision, tempered by a firm sense
of right and wrong. But we cannot assume that he found Marvell a royalist in 1651, and converted him. Marvell was remotely
connected with the Fairfax family, through his stepmother and
others, and he may well have met him in the mysterious 1640s;
certainly his brothers-in-law would have seen him often during
the siege of Hull.[24] Nor is it likely that Fairfax would have
engaged an avowed royalist to teach his only child at an im-
pressionable age. Marvell wrote the 'Horatian Ode' in the

summer of 1650, and though it was not published then, it is
difficult to believe that Fairfax was unaware of it. In 1651, he
also wrote a Latin ode to Oliver St. John on his departure as
ambassador to the Netherlands. (St. John, like Fairfax, had
declined to be associated with Charles I's trial, though he was
then Chief Justice of Common Pleas.) When war broke out with
the Dutch in 1652 he wrote a sharply satirical poem, 'The
Character of Holland', in support of the government line.

This was the first of his satires, and it shows an active dislike
for the Dutch which he must have acquired during his visit in
the 1640s. It was not published until 1665, when the next
Anglo-Dutch war was in full swing, but it was presumably
shown to the men in power, and used to support his application
for a post in the government service, which was supported by
John Milton, Latin Secretary to the government, in a letter to
Bradshaw, President of the Council State, in February 1653.
Milton was a hard-line Puritan, deeply committed to the
Republic; in his *Eikonoklastes* and *The Tenure of Kings and
Magistrates*, in 1649, he had firmly, even boastfully, justified
the execution of Charles I. But it would be unwise to conclude
from this that Marvell shared Milton's views to the full, and
Milton's phraseology does not suggest that he knew him at all
well. He was, he said, 'a man who, both by report and the
converse I have had with him, [is] of singular desert for the state
to make use of'.[25] Almost certainly his prime motive for recommending Marvell as his assistant was simply his fluency in
Latin.

Unfortunately the creation of this additional post was
shelved, and in late 1653 or early 1654 Marvell left Fairfax's
service and took a post as tutor to an orphaned ward of Oliver
Cromwell's, William Dutton. In 1654 he was living with Dutton at Eton, where he would have met some of the most learned
men of the age, notably the Greek scholar John Hales, and John
Oxenbridge, whose experience in the Bermudas may have
inspired Marvell's poem of the same name—though the information he could just as easily have acquired from books. In
1656 he took young Dutton to Saumur, then the intellectual
centre of French Protestantism.[26]

Dutton's guardian was clearly an important man, as was
Mary Fairfax's father, but this should not blind us to the fact

that the post of tutor was a lowly one, especially for a man in his thirties, and one with no future. (It can be compared with the post of governess in Victorian society.) Marvell may or may not have been trying to make a reputation as poet, but he was certainly not publishing anything; here there is a marked contrast between him and Edmund Waller or Richard Lovelace, to mention only two of his contemporaries. He kept in touch with Milton, who in 1654 sent him a copy of his *Defensio Secunda*, a markedly republican tract which Marvell tactfully praised for its 'Roman eloquence'. In the same year Cromwell took over the headship of the state as Lord Protector, and in 1655 Marvell published anonymously 'The First Anniversary of the Government under O.C.'—the only important poem he published in his lifetime. This, together with his 'Horatian Ode upon Cromwell's Return from Ireland', and his poem 'Upon the death of his late Highness the Lord Protector' in 1658 (both unpublished), plus perhaps his poems addressed to Fairfax, are our sole means of assessing his political attitude in the 1650s.

These poems, like everything else Marvell wrote, have been subjected to a very intense examination by our literary theorists,[27] but a few general remarks will not be *mal à propos*. The 'Horatian Ode' is the best and the most anthologized of these poems, and it must have been written some time between Cromwell's return from Ireland in May 1650, having crushed a rebellion which had been smouldering for nearly nine years, and his departure in July to deal similarly with the Scots. It covers in general terms the King's defeat and execution (though not, we notice, his trial); and Marvell's sympathetic treatment of Charles I, particularly in those famous lines:

> *He* nothing common did or mean
> Upon that memorable Scene:
>   But with his keener Eye
>   The Axes edge did try;[28]

has led many scholars into deep disquisitions on his royalist sympathies. I do not doubt that Marvell, like many parliamentarians, felt the tragic wastefulness and pathos of the King's death, but the hero of the poem is Cromwell, and Marvell's treatment of Charles is only intended to point up the contrast between the two men to Cromwell's advantage—after all, there is nothing heroic about defeating a negligible adversary.[29] It is Cromwell who is 'Wars and Fortunes Son', who must 'march indefatigably on'; and as with Fairfax a little later it is his rectitude and his respect for law which is as attractive as his valour and his military skill:

> How good he is, how just,
> And fit for highest Trust:
> Nor yet grown stiffer with Command,
> But still in the *Republick's* hand.[30]

In fact, Cromwell soon outgrew the Republic's hand. In 1653 he forcibly dispersed the Rump of the Long Parliament, and in December of that year assumed the title of Lord Protector under a new Instrument of Government drawn up by the Army Council, inaugurating what can best be described as a constitutional military dictatorship. A year later, as we have seen, Marvell reviewed the situation, in verse.

His poem on 'The First Anniversary' is a paean of unqualified praise; clearly Marvell was far from regarding the Protector's rule as unconstitutional. And whereas he had taken up fully half the 'Horatian Ode' describing and in a sense justifying Cromwell's high-handed treatment of Charles I, he now wasted no time on the unfortunate Long Parliament; Cromwell was simply praised for having taken a short cut to political sanity which was denied to the more ponderous authority of kings:

> 'Tis he the force of scatter'd Time contracts,
> And in one Year the work of Ages acts:
> While heavy Monarchs make a wide Return,
> Longer, and more Malignant than *Saturn*.[31]

In fact, Parliament is conspicuously absent from all these Cromwellian poems, except as a butt for the Protector's ruthless organizing genius:

> Such was that wondrous Order and Consent,
> When *Cromwell* tun'd the ruling Instrument;
> While tedious Statesmen many years did hack,
> Framing a Liberty that still went back.[32]

Yet behind it all was an idea also dimly glimpsed in the 'Horatian Ode', that Cromwell was only the agent of a higher power:

if in some happy Hour
High Grace should meet in one with the highest Pow'r,
And then a seasonable People still
Should bend to his, as he to Heavens will.

Or again:

What since he did [since 1649], and higher Force him push'd
Still from behind, and it before him rush'd,
Though undiscern'd among the tumult blind,
Who think those high-Degrees by Man design'd.[33]

This was a fusion, possibly, of two ideas: the idea of the Davidic hero, the martial spokesman of God's chosen people, and the idea of the Machiavellian Prince, who will secure the state by his exercise of *virtu*, a mixture of military prowess and political dexterity. In both there is the concept of rolling, inevitable military might so evident in Milton's Angels. The idea of militarism as a virtue is so antithetical to our thinking that we tend to reject it out of hand, but it was in fact basic to Western political thought in the seventeenth century. Machiavelli had posited a balanced republican unit, but led by a prince whose spiritual impregnability matched his military virtuosity.[34] It is thus that the Cromwell of Marvell's poems appears, and out of war, brutality, and savagery he would forge a new state:

But thee triumphant hence the firy Carr,
And firy Steeds had born out of the Warr,
From the low World, and thankless Men above,
Unto the Kingdom blest of Peace and Love.[35]

If you were to say that this is akin to Fascism, then you would be right—after all, another name for Fascism was 'romantic authoritarianism'. But the seventeenth century, of course, did not see it that way. Their problem was to find an acceptable substitute for paternal, charismatic monarchical authority within a republican framework, and to men like Marvell Cromwell was the ideal; a God-given military leader who would remould the state while remaining subject to the law.

In such a scenario religion, like parliament, had a minor role. Marvell leaves us in no doubt of his contempt for the sectarian zealots who had tried to stay the course of the Protector's chariot, and his strictures on the Fifth Monarchists in the 'First Anniversary' ode echo his contemptuous dismissal of Dutch sectarianism in 'The Character of Holland'.[36] We know nothing of his religious stance in the 1650s, but, extrapolating from his attitude under Charles II, we are safe in assuming that he was one of those Puritans who took refuge in the loosely-organized state church created in 1655 by Cromwell and his unofficial vice-gerent in spirituals, John Owen.

In the meanwhile Marvell's tutorship presumably brought him into close contact with Cromwell. Only one letter from Marvell to Cromwell survives, reporting on young Dutton's progress at Eton, but there must have been others, particularly from Saumur, and Marvell probably reported to Cromwell face to face. It is almost inconceivable that Cromwell was unfamiliar with the poems we have just been discussing, and that he did not approve them in general terms, though he may have found their praise of him a trifle excessive. It was not to be expected that a man like Marvell, with his political views, his talent for languages and for propaganda poetry, should remain unemployed, and in 1657 he secured the post which had eluded him in 1653, that of Assistant Secretary to Milton, who was now totally blind.

Naturally, it was in Marvell's interest later to play down this episode in his life, and he covered his tracks well. In 1673 he had the nerve to write:

I never had any, not the remotest relation to publick matters, nor correspondence with the persons then predominant, until the year of 1657, when indeed I enter'd into an imployment, for which I was not altogether improper, and which I consider'd to be the most innocent and inoffensive toward his Majestyies affairs of any in that usurped and irregular Government, to which all men were then exposed. And this I accordingly discharg'd without disobliging any one person, there having been opportunity and indeavours since his Majesties happy return to have discover'd [it] had it been otherwise.[37]

This is true in itself, but it is not the whole truth. Undoubtedly Marvell was an intimate of James Harrington, and approved of the republican scheme of government outlined in his *Oceana*, published in 1656. He was a member of the republican Rota Club, and would therefore probably have sympathized with

Milton's *A Ready and Easy Way to Establish a Free Commonwealth*, a bold, almost reckless, republican scenario which was published at the end of 1659 and republished as late as April 1660.

Also it is clear that he was very close to the Protectorial family. In November 1657 he wrote two songs for the wedding of Mary Cromwell to Viscount Fauconberg,[38] and in the ode he wrote on the death of Cromwell a year later he explained at great length how the death of Cromwell's favourite daughter Elizabeth by cancer in August 1658 had precipitated her father's death a month later—a point which would not have been made, I feel, by anyone who was not on intimate terms with the family.[39] Other anxious Cromwellians, like Edmund Waller, with 'Upon the late Storm, and of the death of his Highness ensuing the Same', or John Dryden, with his 'Heroic Stanzas consecrated to the Glorious Memory of his most Serene and Renowned Highness Oliver', did not allude to this point, even indirectly. Even more revealing are the lines:

> I saw him dead, a leaden slumber lyes,
> And mortal sleep over those wakefull eyes.[40]

If we take this literally, as I think we must, then Marvell shared an unusual privilege with Cromwell's family and close friends, for the Protector's body decomposed so fast that it had to be buried 'immediately and in a private manner'. For the solemn lying-in-state at Somerset House a wax effigy was used (announced as such) and a closed but empty coffin.[41] Marvell was also one of a select group which walked alongside this coffin at the formal state funeral—with him were Milton and Dryden, but not Waller—today we would call him a pallbearer.

In his valedictory ode to Cromwell Marvell pledged his support to his son Richard, who succeeded him as Lord Protector, and he was elected to the new parliament summoned for January 1659 as one of the Members for Hull. There is nothing surprising in this. His brother-in-law Edmund Popple was sheriff and returning officer, and no doubt Marvell had kept up his connections in the East Riding, though we cannot prove it.

However, the Cromwellian regime now crashed. Richard was painlessly removed by an army *coup d'état* and his new parliament was dissolved; then the triumphant generals were taken in the back in May 1659 by their junior officers, who demanded the return of the Rump, the remnant of the Long Parliament expelled by Oliver in 1653. The Rump's excesses were such that the Army expelled it again that autumn, only to be outflanked by George Monck, commander-in-chief in Scotland. Monck's intervention led to the return of the Rump, but when he reached London in February 1660 even he found the Rump impossible to work with. He speedily ordered the return of the surviving members of the Long Parliament who had been excluded on 2 December 1648, when this whole hysterical series of events had begun. The reconstituted Long Parliament at once dissolved itself, and summoned another parliament, the Convention, for April 1660. Andrew Marvell was again elected for Hull, together with a staunch Puritan, John Ramsden. The Convention promptly recalled Charles II.

Marvell's position was certainly delicate, but by no means dangerous. He had had nothing to do with Charles I's trial or execution, and this was the cardinal point. If service in the usurping government or writing laudatory poems on its behalf was to be a crime, then thousands were criminals. In any case, only one of Marvell's Cromwellian poems had been published, and that anonymously; Dryden and Waller both published similar effusions under their own name, and not only survived, but survived to be court poets to Charles II. Marvell lost his post in the government, though when we do not know; as late as July 1660 he was drafting a Latin letter to the Elector Palatine on the King's behalf;[42] but his immunity was confirmed by the statesmanlike Act of Indemnity and Oblivion pushed through by the new government in August. He was confident enough, in fact, to turn to the defence of old friends like Milton. Milton spent some months in prison, and there was a call for him to be excluded from the Act of Oblivion. There is a tradition (unfortunately unprovable) that Marvell defended him in the Commons; certainly in December 1660 he had a spirited exchange with the Attorney-General as to whether Milton should pay his prison fees.[43]

In the meanwhile Marvell had been assiduous in the interests of Hull Corporation; ensuring that the professional garrison was disbanded with the rest of Cromwell's army, buttonholing

the Secretary to the Lord Treasurer, Sir Philip Warwick, to
secure Hull an independent excise establishment, and lobbying
vigorously to secure an independent militia establishment,
too.[44] This paid off in January 1661, when he was re-elected to
the famous Cavalier Parliament, which in the event sat until
January 1679, after Marvell's death. This time, however, he
was yoked with Colonel Anthony Gilby, a distinguished
royalist soldier. Gilby was Deputy Governor of Hull, and the
Governor and High Steward was an even more prominent
royalist soldier, Lord Bellasis of Worlaby, and a Roman
Catholic to boot. As early as June 1661 Marvell and Gilby
quarrelled violently over constituency business, but Marvell
said it arose 'from some crudities and undigested matter remaining upon the stomach ever since our election'.[45] This was
patched over, and we find Marvell and Gilby acting in perfect
accord in later years, but in the first few months of 1663 Marvell
absented himself in Holland, for reasons not known, and Bellasis suggested to the corporation that they elect a new Member
(actually they could not have done this without leave of the
House). The Corporation simply asked Marvell to come back,
and in July of the same year he was careful to secure their
permission to go as secretary to the Earl of Carlisle on an
embassy to Russia, Sweden, and Denmark. Originally this was
scheduled to last a year, but it was January 1665 before Marvell
returned. Bellasis was removed in 1673 by the Test Act, and his
place was taken by the young Duke of Monmouth, Charles II's
eldest illegitimate son, who was Lord-Lieutenant of the East
Riding and later Captain-General of the Army.

Marvell was very much a professional M.P. and one of the
last to be paid for his services. In return he gave a full professional service, and his letters are full of his efforts on the
Corporation's behalf, in such matters as wine licences, the
excise, and the discouragement of foreign shipping. The
renewal of the citadel after the depredations of the Civil War,
and the Corporation's financial responsibility therefor, are a
subject to themselves. I am impressed by the strength of the
City's representation in London, and I wonder if other towns
were similarly equipped. Apart from the two M.P.s Hull maintained a 'towns intelligencer', a Mr. Stockdale, and on an
important question, like the future of the garrison, we find all

the town's big guns deployed: Lord Bellasis, Marvell and
Gilby, and Stockdale, all waited on the Lord General, the Duke
of Albemarle, in a body.[46]

As for his share in the business of the House, Marvell himself
said in 1677 that he had spoken 'seldom', and he apologized if he
was 'not so well tuned'.[47] It is true that his name appears rarely
in the diary of Anchitel Grey, covering the years 1667 to 1678
and beyond; but the diary of John Milward, which only covers
the period September 1666 to May 1668, records eight speeches
by Marvell, some of them quite important. This gives a rather
different picture.

In fact, Milward, who was a staunch Anglican Tory, clearly
regarded Marvell as a prominent opposition spokesman, and in
some sense the busy, dutiful, rather pedestrian Member for
Hull who appears in his letters to the Corporation was leading a
double life. His letters to his favourite nephew William Popple,
who went out from Bordeaux in 1670 to handle the French end
of the family wine business, were written in a much franker
vein, and from them we can deduce his disgust and dis-
illusionment with the Restoration establishment.[48] Moreover,
he had already written an important anonymous poem against
the King's government. His 'Last Instructions to a Painter' was
clandestinely published in 1667 under the name of Sir John
Denham, a noted courtier-poet whose wife was in fact pilloried
in it.[49]

The 'Advice-to-a-Painter' form was borrowed from the
Italians by Edmund Waller, whose fawning 'Instructions to a
Painter' in 1666 called upon the artist to depict the heroism of
the King's brother, the Duke of York, in the battle of Lowestoft
on 3 June 1665. This was ruthlessly parodied by Marvell in the
'Last Instructions', which instead called upon the painter to
depict 'this race of drunkards, pimps and fools',[50] who had let
the Navy run down, who had done their best to corrupt Parliament, who were intent on concluding a humiliating peace, and
who by their irresponsibility had made possible the Dutch
attack on Chatham that autumn, one of the most disgraceful
episodes in British naval history.

He was unsparing in his scurrilous violence against certain
courtiers, especially those who were Catholic or Catholic-
orientated, like Henry Jermyn, Earl of St. Albans:

Paint him with *Drayman's* Shoulders, butcher's *Mien*,
Member'd like Mules, with Elephantine chine,[51]

or the King's mistress, the Countess of Castlemaine, whose
weakness for well-hung porters and footmen was graphically
described.[52] He even satirized the physical appearance and
sexual tastes of Anne Hyde, Duchess of York:

> Paint her with Oyster Lip, and breath of Fame,
> Wide Mouth that Sparagus may well proclaim:
> With *Chanc'llor's* Belly and so large a Rump.
> There, not behind the Coach, her Pages jump.[53]

He also visits with withering contempt the smart courtiers who
follow General Monck to Chatham in hopes of a free show, but
leave him to face the fighting alone:

> Our feather'd *Gallants*, which came down that day
> To be Spectators safe of the *new Play,*
> Leave him alone when first they hear the Gun;
> (*Cornbry* the fleetest) and to *London* run.[54]

But this was not a direct attack on Charles II. In fact, though
he was free with Lady Castlemaine, in at least one instance he
seems to have held his hand rather than give personal offence;
while satirizing Lord St. Albans it would have been easy to
dwell on his supposed liaison with the Queen Mother, as many
libellers did. The poem is studded with slighting references to
Charles's courtiers and ministers, but he is not directly blamed
for their conduct, nor (rather more surprisingly) was the Duke
of York or the Earl of Clarendon, though as we have seen, the
Duke's wife, who was also Clarendon's daughter, was held up to
derision. In fact, in October 1667, when Clarendon's
impeachment was under consideration, Marvell twice intervened in an attempt to moderate the Commons' attitude. He
intervened again in an attempt to prevent Peter Pett, the Com-
missioner for Chatham dockyard, being sent to the Tower, and
obviously he thought both men were being made scapegoats for
the sins of others.[55] As more evidence came in his animosity was
focused on Lord Arlington, and in February 1668 he burst out
against him in the Commons 'somewhat transportedly', accus-
ing him of buying the Secretaryship of State for £10,000.
Several Members called on him to explain himself.[56]

As for Charles II, the 'Last Instructions' ends with his

experiencing a warning dream. At first this misfires; the lascivious monarch mistakes the purpose of an allegorical female
nude representing England and Peace, and tries to pull her into
bed; but she evades his grasp and gives way to the ghost of his
father Charles I and his grandfather, Henry IV of France,
assassinated in 1610. Chastened by this reminder that a loyal
people can be provoked too far, he rises from his bed determined on a change of policy. There follows an 'Envoi' in which
the poet calls upon him to rid himself of his unworthy servants,
who have nearly brought him to his ruin and come between
himself and his people. There is more than one way of looking at
this—for instance, it could have saved the author from a change
of seditious libel if discovered—but it is also possible that
Marvell was still seeking the return of the kind of militant,
decisive leadership he had received from Oliver. In other
words, the 'Last Instructions' can be read as a direct appeal to
the King over the heads of his ministers, like Halifax's 'Character of a Trimmer' in 1684.[57]

With Marvell's prose work *The Rehearsal Transpros'd* in 1672,
followed by the 'Second Part' in 1673, we are on safer ground;
up to a point, at least. It was written in response to *A Discourse of
Ecclesiastical Politie*, by Samuel Parker, a rising young Anglican
divine, later to be Bishop of Oxford and a noted collaborator
with James II, who argued strongly against religious toleration
and in favour of the imposition of total conformity by state
decree. Marvell's authorship was no secret, after minor
alterations the tract received a royal imprimatur, and he openly
put his name to the second part.

Marvell had survived the Restoration, presumably, as some
sort of Anglican conformist. His religion remained ambiguous.
As an anonymous pamphleteer said in 1678:

He's a shrewd man against popery, though [as] for his [own] religion,
you may place him as Pasquin placed Henry VIII; betwixt Moses, the
Messiah and Mahomet, with the motto, *Quo me vertam nescio*.[58]

As an M.P., the only statutory requirement imposed on him
was that he should take the oaths of allegiance and supremacy;
in May 1661, however, the new House of Commons voted to go
to St Margaret's, Westminster, and take the Anglican sacrament *en masse*; absentees and laggards were jealously noted,

and the Member for Hull was not amongst them. But this apart, it was very easy for a Londoner to avoid any overt religious commitments, as the diary of Samuel Pepys shows; (Pepys went to church every Sunday, but he never took communion). In fact, in the metropolis church attendance of any kind was virtually unenforceable. In March 1668, in the Commons, Marvell was one of those who fought vigorously and successfully to prevent the renewal of the Conventicles Act against Nonconformists, and when a new bill was introduced in 1670 he fought it again, describing it in a celebrated phrase as 'the quintessence of arbitrary malice'.[59] It would be unwise to assume from this that he was a Nonconformist himself, but he could only greet with approval Charles II's Declaration of Indulgence in March 1672 which suspended the operation of the penal laws. In *The Rehearsal Transpros'd* he held Samuel Parker up to ridicule, argued that his attitude was obscurantist and unchristian, and declared that it was the duty of the magistrate to lead the nation towards toleration.

The sarcastic, punning, involuted way in which the tract is written is infinitely tedious and irritating to our tastes, but it was a style much beloved of the age, and it won him many admirers. Gilbert Burnet thought it one of 'the wittiest books that have appeared in this age', and records that 'from the King down to the tradesman' it was read 'with great pleasure'. In fact, Charles II, never much of a reader, read this book 'over and over again'.[60] It is natural enough that he should, since Marvell was apparently defending precisely the policy he had adopted in the Declaration of Indulgence. There may even be some truth in the unsupported story, first published by Thomas Cooke in 1726, that the King's chief minister, the Earl of Danby, tried to enlist him in the Court party.[61] This could have been in 1673, when Danby had just taken over, and Marvell had recently published the second part of *The Rehearsal Transpros'd* under his own name.

But a detailed analysis of these two pamphlets shows that Marvell was not such an uncritical supporter of the King as at first appears; just as in the 'Last Instructions' his hostility to the King is muted, so now his praise.[62] In the 'Second Part' he made a famous statement on the Great Rebellion which helps define his position:

Whether it were a War of Religion, or of Liberty, is not worth the labour to enquire. Which-soever was at the top, the other was at the bottom; but upon considering all, I think the Cause was too good to have been fought for. Men ought to have trusted God; they ought and might have trusted the King with the whole matter . . . For men may spare their pains where Nature is at work, and the world will not go the faster for our driving. Even as his present Majestie's happy Restauration did it self, so all things else happen in their best and proper time, without any need of our officiousness.[63]

It is difficult to be sure, but this may well have represented Marvell's own view in 1642—or his view as it appeared across the gap of thirty years. Like many of his generation, he had been at a loss because of lack of leadership. He had found that leadership in Cromwell, but only temporarily. The Restoration suggested that the King was God-given, and therefore ought to be endowed with powers of leadership. He was still looking for those powers in Charles II.

What he meant when he said that 'the cause was too good to be fought for' was that Charles I himself ought to have seen the justice of his opponents' claims and himself led the movement for reform. The people individually can reform the government, by reforming themselves; but the people as a whole cannot do this, except by a communal upheaval which is more destructive than allowing the machine to run down. In moments of crisis the role of the monarch is all important, because he alone of men has the power not only to reform himself but to reform the commonwealth. The idea of reform from above was typical of a whole succession of men, from John Pym through Lord Halifax to Robert Walpole, and on to Edmund Burke. This is how Marvell put it:

[A]ll Governments and Societies of men . . . do in process of long time gather an irregularity, and wear away much of their primitive institution. And therefore the true wisdom of all Ages hath been to review at fit periods those errours, defects or excesses, that have insensibly crept on into the Publick Administration; to brush the dust off the Wheels, and oyl them again, or if it be found advisable to chuse a set of new ones. And this Reformation is most easily and with least disturbance to be effected by the Society it self, no single men being forbidden by any Magistrate to amend their own manners, and much more all Societies having the liberty to bring themselves within compass. But if men themselves shall omit their duty in this matter, the only just and lawful way remains by the Magistrate, who, having the greatest trust and interest in preserving the publick welfare, had need take care to redress in good season whatsoever corruptions that may indanger and infect the Government. Otherwise, if the Society it self shall be so far from correcting its own exorbitances, as to defend them even to the offence and invasion of the Universality; and if Prince's shall not take the advantage of their errours to reduce them to reason; this work, being on both sides neglected, falls to the Peoples share, from which God defend every good Government.[64]

But in fact Charles II was not the paladin which Marvell had only half expected him to be. Even while Marvell wrote the second part of *The Rehearsal Transpros'd* it had become obvious that the King's motives in signing the Declaration of Indulgence had not been entirely disinterested. Suspicion grew that it had all been a conspiracy by the papists, assisted by Louis XIV of France. Evidence was lacking, and though Charles was forced by Parliament to cancel his Declaration of Indulgence in 1673, the following year he was prudent enough to withdraw from the war. Unfortunately, by this time it was apparent that the Duke of York, heir presumptive to the throne, was a Roman Catholic, and from 1674 onwards Charles and Danby began to build a new Anglican monarchy, monolithic and persecuting, which also seemed nothing but a front for Catholicism.

Naturally, in the 1670s Marvell was a leading member of the Country Party; for one thing this was the natural resting place for the Harringtonian or Machiavellian republicans left over from the 1650s. It has even been suggested that he so far overcame his antipathy to the Dutch as to join in the propaganda campaign against the English government organized by William III. But this hinges on the presence of his name in certain lists and we must remember that in 1671 Sir Thomas Osborne (later Earl of Danby) included him in a list of 'such as may be engaged by the Duke of York and his friends', which is unlikely to say the least.[65] His aversion to Roman Catholicism and to establishment Anglicanism if anything increased. In March 1677 he violently opposed a bill sent down by the Lords to regularize the situation if the next king was a Catholic; no doubt he realized that to regularize a situation was to prepare

the way for it. But he was particularly excited by the proviso
that in such an event all ecclesiastical preferment should be
controlled by the bishops. 'Whether this bill will prevent popery or not', he said, 'it will secure the promotion of the
bishops'.[66] His conduct brought down on him the censure of
the Speaker, Edward Seymour, and the next time he came into
the House he stumbled, and fell against Sir Philip Warwick.
Seymour tried to represent this as a deliberate assault, and it is
interesting to see how the sides lined up: on Marvell's side were
Sir Henry Capel, Sir Robert Howard, Joseph Garroway, and
Sir Thomas Meres, all prominent members of the Country
Party. He was also friendly in 1677 and 1678 with Sir Edward
Harley of Brampton Bryan, a noted Puritan, and the father of
Robert Harley.[67]

On the other hand, there is no reason why he should not have
been personally known to Charles II, as some rather weak
eighteenth-century authorities suggest. An M.P. was an important man, much more so than today. In the 1660s London high
society, including the House of Lords, the Commons and those
few courtiers who belonged to neither, numbered less than a
thousand. This exclusiveness was enhanced by the fact that
Charles kept the same Parliament from 1661 to 1679; by the
1670s the surviving Members must have been very familiar figures. And Marvell was a familiar figure in another way,
for a man who was a close friend of those notorious and unre-
pentant republicans John Milton and John Harrington must
have been under government surveillance, even if it was inter-
mittent.[68]

His last authenticated work was *An Account of the Growth of
Popery and Arbitrary Power in England*, published late in 1677,
in which he forcefully argued that there was a conspiracy afoot
between Louis XIV, the Jesuits, and the English Catholics to
subvert Protestantism and constitutional government. It began
with the commanding words:

There has now for divers years a design been carried on, to change the
lawful government of England into an absolute tyranny, and to con-
vert the established Protestant Religion into downright Popery; than
both which, nothing can be more destructive or contrary to the
interest and happiness, to the Constitution and being of the King and
Kingdom.

Marvell's suspicions of Catholicism were wildly exaggerated, but the general reaction to the Popish Plot a year later shows that his views were common enough. The pamphlet was much admired in Whig circles, then and later, and roused a corresponding anger in the government, which in March 1678 offered a reward for the discovery of the printer or author. Yet, true to his previous policy, Marvell was careful to absolve the King from blame, and even the Duke of York and the Earl of Danby. It was much harsher in tone than his previous works, but it can still be read as a last desperate appeal for national unity under a reformed monarchy.[69]

What kind of man he was, we scarcely know. We only have John Aubrey's word that 'he was of middling stature, pretty strong set, roundish faced, cherry cheeked, [with] hazel eye[s]'. Aubrey goes on to say that 'he was in his conversation very modest, and of few words; and though he loved wine he would never drink hard in company'. In fact, he preferred to drink alone, which is perhaps a trifle sinister; 'he kept bottles of wine at his lodging, and many times he would drink liberally by himself to refresh his spirits and exalt his muse'.[70] All we can add to this is the fact that his few recorded interventions on parliamentary debates, in 1667, 1668, and 1677, suggest a man of violent emotions, not quite in command of himself.[71] Aubrey tells us that 'he had not a general acquaintance', though his close friends included James Harrington, as we have seen, and Milton. He wrote a commendatory poem for the second edition of 'Paradise Lost', in 1674, and put his initials to it.[72] He never married, though latterly he had a housekeeper, Mary Palmer, who falsely claimed to be his widow, and brought out the first edition of his poems in 1681.

He had substantial lodgings in Maiden Lane, Covent Garden, within easy reach of Westminster, and at one time a house in Highgate; it is difficult to sustain the myth of genteel poverty put about by his early biographers, who, having awarded him a substantial fortune in the 1640s, absentmindedly deprive him of it in the 1670s. But how he supported himself remains a mystery. Hull Corporation paid him 6s. 8d. a day for his services, and at first glance this seems handsome enough, until we remember that it was only paid during parliamentary sessions, which under Charles II were brief and widely spaced. For instance, Parliament did not meet from 23 April 1671 to 4 February 1673, nor from 23 November 1675 to 15 February 1677; and on only two occasions, in 1661–2 and 1677–8, did it sit for more than six months on any one calendar year.

However, the efforts of scholars to solve the problem of Mary Palmer—whether she was Marvell's wife, and if not, why she said she was—have given us a new insight into Marvell's financial circumstances. It now appears that he was closely involved with an overseas trading firm founded in 1671 by Edward Nelthorpe and Richard Thompson. Thompson was a cousin of Marvell's on his mother's side, and letters survive from Marvell to his brother Edward Thompson of York, also a merchant. Nelthorpe was a distant cousin of them both, and all three were close friends.[73] In 1676 the firm went bankrupt, and in 1677 Marvell took additional lodgings in Great Russell Street, where he sheltered his friends from their creditors; he also underwrote a £500 bond of Nelthorpe's. Marvell's death, followed only a month later by Nelthorpe's, was the cause of considerable embarrassment, and Mary Palmer's claim to be Mrs. Marvell was a legal fiction, entered into with Nelthorpe's creditors, in order to secure the £500 from Marvell's estate. In fact, it looks as though the publication of his poems in 1681, when the case was still before the courts, was designed not only to increase the value of the estate but also to confirm Mary's status as his widow.

In the long-drawn-out proceedings in the courts it was asserted that Marvell was 'at several times for several years before his death kept and maintained' by Nelthorpe and Thompson. Also it was deposed that he 'was not for the space of five years before he died worth £100 at any time', and that on his death his estate was 'not on the whole worth £30'.[74] These witnesses had an axe to grind, but it is reasonable to suppose that Marvell had some financial interest in his cousins' firm, which must have been damaged when it crashed in 1676. The phrase 'at several times for several years' is also interesting. Perhaps the firm subsidized Marvell during parliamentary recesses in return for his services as a lobbyist? We do not know. However, it does seem likely that he died in embarrassed circumstances, if not actual poverty.

Death came suddenly, on 18 August 1678, shortly after his

last visit to Hull; suddenly enough to provoke the usual rumours of poison, though they have long been disproved, if this were necessary. He was buried in St. Giles-in-the-Fields. The legend that his memorial tablet was removed by royalists, presumably in the 1680s, or that its installation was forbidden by the rector, John Sharp, can be dismissed.[75] But certainly there is a mystery about his memorial. Hull Corporation voted the very considerable sum of £50 'towards the discharge of his funeral and to perpetuate his memory by a grave stone',[76] which suggests that they did not regard Marvell as particularly wealthy. It is not clear that any such gravestone was put up, and it would not surprise me if Mary Palmer and her associates appropriated the money. Thomas Cooke printed an epitaph in 1726, and a slightly amended version was installed in St. Giles by one of Marvell's descendants, Robert Nettleton, in 1764.

Andrew Marvell's reputation on his death, and for a century after it, is difficult to assess. It is far below that which we would think appropriate for a man whose poetry is now so much admired; yet far above what we would expect from the meagre facts of his life as we know them. It is the case of the whole being greater than the sum of the parts.

When the Whig publicist Thomas Cooke came to edit his *Complete Works* in 1726 he announced, 'My design in this is to draw a pattern for all free-born Englishmen in the life of a worthy patriot, whose every action has truly merited to him, with Aristides, the surname of the Just'. From his works he hoped to draw 'a complete system of sound and wholesome doctrines . . . such as must certainly reproach the age for having been so much neglected'. His purpose was to describe for posterity Marvell's resolute opposition to the government of Charles II as a Member of Parliament and a party propagandist, a bias reflected in his epitaph. This records that he served in Parliament 'with such wisdom, dexterity, integrity and courage as becomes a true patriot', and that his 'most peculiar graces of wit and learning', his 'singular penetration and strength of judgment', and his 'unalterable steadiness in the ways of virtue', made him 'the ornament and example of his age'. But 'his inimitable writings' were only mentioned as an afterthought, and the reference even then is probably to his prose, not his verse. When he turned to his poetry Thomas Cooke was almost condescending:

There are few of his poems which have not something pleasing in them, and some he must be allowed to have excelled in. Most of them seem to have been the effect of a lively genius, and manly sense, but at the same time seem to want that correctness he was capable of making. If we have any which may be said to have come finished from his hands, they are these; *On Milton's Paradise Lost, On Blood's Stealing the Crown,* and *A Dialogue between Two Horses.*[77]

It is necessary always to remember, in fact, that very few of his political poems were published in his lifetime, and the only important one (on Cromwell's first anniversary) was published anonymously. The folio edition of 1681 did not include this or his other two Cromwellian poems. Indeed, these were unknown even to Thomas Cooke, and were first published by Edward Thompson in 1776. His lyrics were in a mode then becoming unfashionable, and more notice seems to have been taken of his satires; the 'Last Instructions to a Painter', and many other 'Instructions' fathered on him after the Revolution.[78] He was also renowned as an opponent of episcopacy because of *The Rehearsal Transpros'd*; in the preface to 'Religio Laici' in 1682, Dryden punningly refers to Martin Marprelate as 'the first Presbyterian scribbler' and 'the Marvell of those times'.[79] This tradition was kept alive by his eighteenth-century biographers, and it was in this spirit that Wordsworth wrote his famous sonnet:

> Great men have been among us; hands that penn'd
> And tongues that utter'd wisdom—better none:
> The later Sidney, Marvell, Harrington,
> Young Vane, and others who called Milton friend.
> These moralists could act and comprehend:
> They knew how genuine glory was put on;
> Taught us how rightfully a nation shone
> In splendour: what strength was, that would not bend
> But in magnanimous meekness.

Yet as late as 1864 the historian of Hull could remark that 'the poems and other works of Marvell are little known and almost inaccessible'.[80]

In fact, there was a very mild boom in Marvell in the second half of the nineteenth century. His *Poetical Works* were reprinted in Boston, Massachusetts, in 1857—the first edition claiming to be comprehensive since 1792—and this was reprinted in London in 1870. He then began to be republished in the kind of pocket collections intended for working men: in 'The Muses' Library' in 1892, and 'The Little Library' in 1904. All the same, it was a bold decision, bolder than we realize, for Hull Corporation to decide to celebrate the tercentenary of Marvell's birth in 1921, and it is worth noting that the Tercentenary Committee was dominated by men who were later closely associated with the founding of the University College, like T. R. Ferens and Malet Lambert. They went the whole hog, with a service in Holy Trinity, a grand luncheon followed by a public lecture, and a special exhibition in the local museum—they even decorated the trams with Marvell motifs.[81]

All the same, their activities must have seemed rather 'babu'. Hensley Henson of Durham, then the most celebrated bishop in the Church of England, delivered a sermon on 'Puritan Citizenship' to the text of Ecclesiasticus 10:25, ('Free men shall minister unto a wise servant, and a man that hath knowledge will not murmur thereat'), which is still worth reading. But they invited as guest lecturer that rather pathetic figure Augustine Birrell, and it is significant that he was probably the best man they could get. He was a superficial essayist and reviewer (the word 'Birrelling' was coined in the 1880s to characterize his output) who in 1905 wrote a shallow pot-boiler on Marvell for the 'English Men of Letters' series. He also had claims to be a second-rank politician, but he had the misfortune to be Chief Secretary in Ireland from 1907 to 1916, when he was comprehensively disgraced. He gave a flamboyant but very silly lecture.

The then Lord Mayor, a character familiar to those who live in northern cities, told the luncheon party that this was 'the biggest and cheapest advertisement that to my knowledge the city has ever experienced', worldly sentiments for which he was suitably reproved by Archdeacon Lambert, and the Committee must have been relieved to notice a challenging revisionist essay on Marvell, by a young American called Eliot, in the *TLS* that week.[82] They hastily sought permission to include it in their tercentenary volume. With Eliot's essay, and Margoliouth's definitive edition of the poems in 1927, the present boom in Marvell may be said to have begun.

NOTES

1. A. B. Grosart (ed.), *The Complete Works of Andrew Marvell*, 4 vols, 1872 (repr. 1966), vol. I, pp. xix–xx, [henceforward cited as 'Grosart']; Pierre Legouis, *Andrew Marvell: Poet, Puritan, Patriot* (Oxford, 1965), p. 1, [henceforward cited as 'Legouis']. Factual details for which no reference is given are taken from Sir Charles Firth's article in the *Dictionary of National Biography*.

2. ll.305–8, H. M. Margoliouth (ed.), *The Poems and Letters of Andrew Marvell*, 3rd ed., revised by P. Legouis and E. E. Duncan Jones, 2 vols (Oxford, 1971), I, 72, [henceforward cited as 'Margoliouth']. See also Elizabeth Story Donno (ed.), *Andrew Marvell: the Complete Poems*, Penguin English Poets (1972), p. 85, [henceforward cited as 'PEP'].

3. Margoliouth, II, 2.

4. John Lawson, *A Town Grammar School through Six Centuries* (Oxford, 1963), p. 83.

5. Lawson, loc. cit.; H. M. Margoliouth, 'Andrew Marvell: some biographical points', *Modern Language Review*, XVII (1922), 351–2.

6. Margoliouth, I, 104–7; PEP, pp. 117–25.

7. Grosart, vol. I, p. xxxvii, vol. III, p. 322; Aubrey, *Brief Lives*, ed. Andrew Clark, 2 vols. (Oxford, 1898), II, 53.

8. *The Rehearsal Transpros'd*, ed. D. I. B. Smith (Oxford, 1971), pp. 203–4.

9. This was rectified by a private Act of 1661, which the younger Marvell worked hard to put through; Margoliouth, II, 24, 30–1; *Victoria County History: East Riding*, i, 287.

10. *VCH*, I, 97–8, 289.

11. 'On General Councils', 1676, Grosart, I, 125.

12. 'A Poem upon the death of O.C.', l.179, Margoliouth, I, 133; PEP, p. 153.

13. J. H. Sheehan, *A History and Description of Hull* (1864), p. 240.

14. Grosart, vol. I, p. xxxiii; Legouis, p. 7; L. N. Wall, 'Marvell and the Skinners', *Notes & Queries*, 207 (1962), 219.

15. H. M. Margoliouth, art. cit. (see n. 5 above); *Andrew Marvell Tercentenary Exhibition: Descriptive Catalogue* (Hull Museum, 1921), item 79.

16. See p. 12 above.

17. John Stoye, *English Travellers Abroad 1604–1667* (1952), p. 303.

18. See the discussion on this poem in Margoliouth, I, 432–5. It is welcomed into the canon by Professor Donno, PEP, p. 227.

19. Margoliouth, I, 2–5; PEP, pp. 47–9.
20. Stoye, op. cit., p. 365ff.
21. H. M. Margoliouth, in *Times Literary Supplement*, 5 June 1924; L. N. Wall, art. cit.
22. John M. Wallace, *Destiny his Choice: The Loyalism of Andrew Marvell* (Cambridge, 1968), ch. 6, [hereafter cited as 'Wallace']. But see Legouis' comment, in Margoliouth, I, 280: 'During the last decade several allegorical interpretations of this poem have been offered, to my mind quite unnecessarily; they are more or less incompatible with one another and at some points palpably impossible. The composition of this poem, in spite of recent ingenious apologies, still seems to me loose, and the tone chatty, except at rare moments of exaltation.'
23. Margoliouth, I, 69; PEP, p. 83.
24. Pauline Burdon, *Andrew Marvell: Some Biographical Background* (School of Languages: Central London Polytechnic, 1975).
25. Grosart, vol. I, p. xxvii. (I think it is clear that Milton is relying on what Marvell himself had told him about his doings in the 1640s, and the fact that he does not mention Marvell's 'war record' is perhaps significant.)
26. Legouis, pp. 105–8.
27. Wallace, chs. 2–3, and other critics there cited.
28. ll.57–60, Margoliouth, I, 93; PEP, p. 56.
29. Christopher Hill suggests that Marvell witnessed the execution; 'Society and Andrew Marvell', in *Puritanism and Revolution* (1958), p. 360. But he could just as easily have obtained all the facts he needed from accounts published in 1649.
30. ll.79–82, Margoliouth, I, 93; PEP, p. 57.
31. ll.13–16, Margoliouth, I, 108–9; PEP, p. 126.
32. ll.67–70, Margoliouth, I, 110; PEP, p. 128.
33. ll.131–4, and 239–42, Margoliouth, I, 114; PEP, pp. 130, 132.
34. J. G. A. Pocock, *The Machiavellian Moment* (Princeton, 1975), pp. 378–83; idem, *The Political Works of James Harrington* (Cambridge, 1977), pp. 16ff.; J. A. Mazzeo, 'Cromwell as Machiavellian Prince in Marvell's "An Horatian Ode"', *Renaissance and Seventeenth-Century Studies* (1964), pp. 166–82. Edmund Waller shared much the same view, he wrote: 'Still as you rise the state, exalted too,/Finds no distemper while 'tis changed by you.' He also took a jaundiced view of the Long Parliament, and comparing Cromwell with Julius Caesar he wrote: 'If Rome's great senate could not wield that sword/Which of the conquered world had made them lord,/What hope had ours, while yet their power was new,/To rule victorious armies but by you?'. See 'A Panegyric to My Lord Protector', ll.141–2, 157–60, in *Silver Poets of the Seventeenth Century*, ed. G. J. A. Parfitt (1974), p. 24.
35. ll.215–18, Margoliouth, I, 114; PEP, p. 132.
36. 'First Anniversary', ll.293–320, Margoliouth, I, 116; PEP, p. 134; 'Character of Holland', Margoliouth, I, 101–2, PEP, pp. 113–14.
37. *The Rehearsal Transpros'd ... Second Part*, ed. D. I. B. Smith (Oxford, 1971), p. 203.

38. Margoliouth, I, 125; PEP, pp. 144–8.
39. ll.29–78, Margoliouth, I, 130–31, PEP, pp. 149–50.
40. ll.247–8, Margoliouth, I, 135; PEP, p. 155.
41. Antonia Fraser, *Cromwell: Our Chief of Men* (1973), pp. 680–82.
42. Legouis, p. 118.
43. *Parliamentary History*, I, 162; Christopher Hill, *Milton and the English Revolution* (1977), p. 208.
44. Margoliouth, II, 2, 16, 18, 19, 20.
45. ibid., 27.
46. ibid., 61–3.
47. Anchitel Grey, *Debates of the House of Commons . . .*, 10 vols, (1763), IV, 330 (29 March 1977), [henceforward cited as 'Grey'].
48. Margoliouth, II, 313–57 *passim*. Popple, who had to return to England in 1685, there made a modest but solid reputation as a political and religious radical. See Caroline Robbins, 'Absolute Liberty: the life and thought of William Popple 1638–1708', *William & Mary Quarterly*, XXIV (1967), 190–223.
49. Some editors also attributed to Marvell the 'Second' and the 'Third Advice to a painter' (1666). There is a case to be made here; their approach is very much the same, unlike the 'Fourth' and 'Fifth Advice', which can certainly be excluded from the canon. But when literary scholars of the eminence of George de Forest Lord, Elizabeth Story Donno, the late H. M. Margoliouth and Margoliouth's modern revisers are in disagreement, a historian must be wary. See de Forest Lord, *Poems on Affairs of State*, vol, I (Yale, 1963), pp. 20–1 and notes; Donno in PEP, pp. 217–18, 279–80; and Margoliouth, I, 347–50.
50. l.12, Margoliouth, I, 147; PEP, p. 157.
51. ll.33–4, Margoliouth, I, 148; PEP, p. 158.
52. ll.79–102, Margoliouth, I, 149; PEP, p. 159.
53. ll.61–4, Margoliouth, I, 148–9; PEP, p. 158. With a pathos which is the height of satire he portrays this ugly, unsatisfied woman lying alone late at night while her husband rides off: 'And nightly hears the hated guards, away/Galloping with the Duke to other prey', (ll.77–8).
54. ll.597–600, Margoliouth, I, 162; PEP, p. 172. (Lord Cornbury was Clarendon's eldest son.)
55. Grey, I, 14, 36; *The Diary of John Milward*, ed. C. Robbins (Cambridge, 1938), pp. 86, 108, 328. Cf. the passage on Pett in 'Last Instructions', ll.765–90, Margoliouth, I, 167; PEP, p. 177.
56. Grey, I, 70–71; Milward's Diary, p. 185.
57. Wallace, pp. 178–83.
58. *Calendar of State Papers Domestic 1678*, p. 122 (18 April 1678).
59. Milward's *Diary*, pp. 225, 338; Margoliouth, II, 301.
60. Gilbert Burnet, *History of My Own Times*, 6 vols (Oxford, 1833), I, 478; H. C. Foxcroft, *Supplement to Burnet's History* (Oxford, 1902), p. 216.
61. Grosart, vol. I, p. xlix.
62. Wallace, pp. 184–207; also Dean M. Schmitter, *Andrew Marvell . . . A Study in the Ecclesiastical and Political Thought of the Restoration* (Columbia Ph.D. dissertation, 1955), ch.2.

63. *The Rehearsal Transpros'd*, ed. cit., p. 135.
64. ibid., pp. 239–40.
65. K. H. D. Haley, *William of Orange and the English Opposition 1672–4* (Oxford, 1953), pp. 57–9; A. Browning, *Thomas Osborne Earl of Danby* 3 Vols (Glasgow, 1944–51), III, 38. L. N. Wall, 'Marvell and the Third Dutch War', *Notes & Queries*, 202 (1957), 296–7, merely shows that Marvell was friendly with a wealthy Dutch immigrant family settled at Hackness, near Scarborough, whose then head, Abram van den Bempde, was arrested by the government on suspicion at the beginning of the war. It is more interesting for the light it throws on Marvell's relations with the merchant aristocracy and with Yorkshire landowners.
66. Grey, IV, 324.
67. ibid., 328–31; Margoliouth, II, 351–7.
68. There is a report in the papers of Sir Joseph Williamson, Arlington's Under-Secretary, in 1671, of Marvell's being involved with a group of 'fanatics' associated with the Duke of Buckingham; *Calendar of State Papers Domestic 1671*, p. 496.
69. Legouis, pp. 154–60; Wallace, p. 207ff.
70. Aubrey, *Brief Lives*, II, 53–4.
71. Legouis also makes this point, p. 138.
72. Margoliouth, II, 137–9; PEP, pp. 192–3.
73. Fred S. Tupper, 'Mary Palmer, alias Mrs Andrew Marvell', *PMLA*, 53 (1938), 367–92, and L. N. Wall, 'Marvell's friends in the City', *Notes & Queries*, 204 (1959), 204–7.
74. Tupper, art. cit., p. 374n.
75. Legouis, p. 224.
76. Not just for 'a monument', as Legouis has it, loc. cit. See Grosart, vol. I, p. xlvii.
77. *Complete Works* (1726), I, 2, 18, 35.
78. See n. 48 above.
79. Dryden, *Poems and Plays*, ed. James Kinsley (Oxford, 1963), p. 279.
80. Sheehan, op. cit., p. 630.
81. *Andrew Marvell: Tercentenary Tributes*, ed. W. H. Bagguley (Oxford, 1921).
82. *Times Literary Supplement*, 31 March 1921.

II

NATURAL MAGIC AND POPULISM IN MARVELL'S POETRY

by WILLIAM EMPSON

THREE hundred years should be long enough to make up our minds; we now seem to have arrived at an orthodox opinion about Marvell, but at the cost of ignoring the old opinion altogether. He is now a very perfect or triple-distilled kind of poet, always seeing round a question; John Carey[1] has written he was like the painter Vermeer, who was working at about the same period and not thought at all special, but two centuries later was found to be glowing from within, holding some secret which made him unique. It is not a very recent opinion; at the tercentenary of his birth, not quite sixty years ago, practically all the things we say now were being said, and I would like to recall a fine sentence on that occasion by Edward Wright, a promising critic who died soon after. He said that Marvell 'expressed into poetry a philosophy as large as that which Coleridge could not render into prose. He was a singing Cambridge Platonist.' A lot of people since then have said something like that, but I think he did it first, and it was never said better. Otherwise the chief thing to recall about 1921 is that some of the trams of Hull were decorated for the occasion. How plain it is that one could not do that to a bus; it would seem very out of place. Those times of innocence are past.

The parallel with Vermeer breaks down because Vermeer when discovered was not already famous for something else. If Hull gave Marvell a centenary celebration in 1778, as may well have happened, he would have been praised as an untiringly useful M.P., an incorruptible fighter for liberty, who also kept up the spirits of his faction, at a risk to himself, in dark times, by fierce but coarsely jovial lampoons. This picture of him is hard to reconcile with the exquisite retiring poet, at his best when praising Nature in solitude. And one cannot quite escape from the Satires by saying that they were written as a painful duty, obviously against the grain, in the last ten years of his life; they are mixed confusingly with bad work by other hands, but some extremely good poetry, very typical of Marvell, is tucked away there. The two sides of him need fitting together somehow, and the clumsy term 'populism' seems to give a line of connection.

The whole title of this lecture is rather clumsy; but it was meant to convey that I shall be discussing the great Nature-poems and also the Satires, while looking for a point of contact between them. For this one must first consider the experiences and convictions of the poet. We are usually told that after leaving Cambridge without an M.A., owing to the death of his father, he became tutor to a rich man's son who went on the Grand Tour all through the Civil War. But no one has found who the pupil can have been; these special tours were much gossiped about—if Marvell went on a secret one he was unique. Besides, if he had wanted to go in for teaching he would surely have taken his M.A. It would have cost very little; there were only a few months still to go, and he had dining rights in his college. The main fact about Marvell's situation, when his father got drowned, was that his two sisters had both married merchant princes of Hull. Such men would regard it as hardly more than a practical precaution to get the in-law decently started in life, all the more as there were no younger sons growing up to demand help in their turn. We hear of Marvell running away to London to join some Jesuits, and being caught there by his father, who lugged him back to Cambridge to go on with his lessons. This implies strong religious feelings but also unsettled ones; he might well not have wanted to become an Anglican country parson, which would have been the probable result of taking his M.A. But he was always fairly canny; the M.A. was a kind of passport, and he would not have given it up unless offered an equally lasting alternative. Surely it is obvious that Edmund Popple offered to take him into the family firm (I leave out the other brother-in-law, Blaydes, because he is never mentioned in the letters; maybe he was already near retirement). We are told of a tradition that the poet 'served his clerkship in Hull', and I do not see why it is ignored; Edmund would naturally make that a first condition. He would say: 'What do you want an M.A. for? You ought to be joining us. First you must spend about a year in the office in Hull, learning the ropes; then you can go abroad. I will see you don't starve.' It would have had to be expressed vaguely and roughly, because one could not tell how the boy would turn out; but actually Popple would have been needing someone like Marvell very much. This was in 1641, just before the Civil War began, and when Hull was still recovering from a severe epidemic of plague. During the Civil War it was twice besieged (refusing entry to the King), and it would be hard to find Hull men free to go and handle the shipping trade in the ports of western Europe. Whether Hull was open at all was a thing that Europe would need to be reassured about (it was always open to receive supplies). Marvell would have had to be prepared to do the actual deskwork, in the English factory at Bordeaux or elsewhere, till the replacement man arrived, but he was a relief-man only, not looking for a settled job, often reporting possibilities or taking letters from one port to another. He came back as soon as the war was over because he was then at last released from doing this emergency work. The emergency had clearly left him enough time to learn four languages and acquire a lot of information. When Cromwell died, about ten years later, Marvell was elected M.P. for Hull, and a first stage in the process was to make him a freeman of the city; he was formally recommended to the Corporation as having already done good service for Hull. But how could he possibly have done good service for Hull, if he had only translated from one language to another, mostly for his rich pupils and then briefly for Cromwell? How could he even know what they wanted him to do?

A reason for supposing he was a tutor from 1642 to 1647, I must recognize, is that he became one from 1650 to 1657. But both these later appointments were political; they kept him within earshot of the sources of power. To tutor a prospective son-in-law of Cromwell, while in line for a post as Secretary for Foreign Languages, and doing various propaganda jobs, was very unlike the ordinary job of bearleader; and, earlier on, to have won the good opinion of General Fairfax, while nominally tutoring his daughter, was a thing that Milton could mention while recommending him to Bradshaw. Marvell had refused to sign up as a regular member of Popple's firm precisely because he wanted to be independent and free for higher things. But to talk about his ambition may give a false impression; it was of a very modest sort. He was a natural 'back-room boy'; he wanted

to be the man on the committee who stopped them from doing
the fatal thing. And not even this degree of ambition could have
occurred to him when he agreed to go north as tutor to Fairfax's
daughter. Somebody must have planned it for him as a rescue
operation, and sprung it upon him with a scolding when he felt
low; he is so very committed before, and the change is quick.
He had arrived back in England firmly supporting the side
which had already lost the war; he wrote elegies for dead
Cavaliers. There is a phrase of grudging respect for the Yorkshireman, General Fairfax, who is only said to be deceived, but
it is clear that Marvell thinks him hopelessly on the wrong side.
Marvell had been shown the poems of Lovelace before they
were printed, and asked to write one of the introductory poems,
which shows that he was recognized by the Cavaliers, who were
still glamorous. His best piece of writing at this time is on the
death of Tom May, a poet who had recently written on the
Parliament side, for money of course, and as a reward, when he
died of being strangled by his muffler while drunk, had a burial
in Westminster Abbey. The reason for insisting on the drink, I
take it, is that propagandists have to drink when at work, in
order to tell lies with the needed air of conviction.

> Poor Poet thou, and grateful Senate they,
> Who thy last Reckoning did so largely pay.
> And with the publick gravity would come,
> When thou hadst drunk thy last to lead thee home.

This is what Dryden has been so rightly praised for; the opponent is totally ridiculed, but he is put in the distance, as another
strange and pathetic example of the fates of men. Still, Dryden
was not doing it till thirty years later. Tom May died in
November 1650, and by early March 1651 Marvell was writing
a Latin epigram to congratulate a Government official on an
appointment to go and negotiate with the Dutch. It is agreed
that Marvell had got to Appleton House by then, and presumably Fairfax had suggested this bit of politeness. He is
thoroughly committed when he gets back to London, two years
later, and shows it by an angry joke against the Dutch, in early
1653. Hull had came out strongly for Parliament in the Civil
War, and Marvell's father had been a Calvinist, so he would be
expected to be on that side. His generosity, and perhaps his

contrariness, had been what made him join the losers, we may feel sure; but he would need to impute worse motives, before he agreed to abandon this wild piece of self-sacrifice. Alas, he would say (as in 'The Coronet'), 'I find the Serpent old'. He had been trying to flaunt himself as a romantic aristocrat; this idea would make him feel free to change, but a friend would have to give the push, by fixing up the almost magical cure of the isolation hospital at Appleton House. The Parliament side was short of good writers, and no wonder they thought Marvell worth saving. But the degree of success can hardly have been expected. He immediately stopped being in love with dead Cavalier heroes; he fell in love with Nature and mixed farming.

While actually on the coach from London, I think, he would have remembered a similar occasion about ten years before, when his father had extracted him from the den of Jesuits and returned him to Cambridge. Again he would feel ashamed of what he had done and yet indignant at being allowed practically no choice; he would perhaps be surly, but within he would feel a vast relief. He had got himself into an almost hopeless jam, and now the more distant prospects, at any rate, were clear again; he would not really mind working for the honest side. He was still not quite thirty. But perhaps one should not allow him much indulgence for that—his sisters did not; this (it seems likely) was when they decided that he would always be unreliable, always prone to be a drag. His whole career, one should remember, was based upon their successful marriages; but they are never once mentioned in any of his letters.

I turn now to 'The Garden' and 'Upon Appleton House', and will assume that he wrote them while with Fairfax. So far as we know, he never tried to print them, or even showed them about; but he would at least have shown them to Fairfax, as they are designed to please him, and appear to have succeeded in this. Fairfax was translating into English, among other things, to occupy his retirement, a commentary by Foix upon *Hermes Trismegistus*, a very basic work of occultism, which says a great deal about the spirits which underlie the operations of Nature. Also he had the poet under observation; it would be like one of those house-parties which decide whether you are accepted for the Foreign Office. The situation of the poet was complex; but it was anyway a situation that made the first verse of 'The

Garden' seem particularly impudent. An air of boyish pluck is one of the most attractive features of this poetry—as has, I think, been said, though not often. Nothing depresses a father more than a son in his twenties who says: 'I don't need to study for a profession, or earn money or anything like that. I can get all the experience I need by just sitting in this garden. And what's more, I don't want to be bothered with girls either.' The mystical renunciation had of course great claims, as Marvell fully realized; but he would also have realized something in between the conflicting ideals. Part of his mind would be saying: 'What a marvellous bit of luck. This place looks frightfully dull, but really it is a springboard. From here one could become somebody, a heeded voice in the secret councils of the Revolution.' This hope he keeps hidden: but he sees no reason to hide his recognition that it is socially a very smart garden, implying power behind the puritanical reserve. There is some paradox also behind his next line of joke: that the gods were only pretending to want to rape the nymphs, whereas really they were trying to make immortal art-works:

> *Apollo* hunted *Daphne* so,
> Only that She might Laurel grow.
> And *Pan* did after *Syrinx* speed,
> Not as a Nymph, but for a Reed.

Well then, the gods had not renounced all effort to win admiration—as they were advised to do in Verse One.

Immediately after this elegant bit of fun Marvell becomes captivated by the garden, and all worldly ideas become impossible to him; he is swept away into an entirely different style.

> What wond'rous Life in this I lead!
> Ripe Apples drop about my head;
> The Luscious Clusters of the Vine
> Upon my Mouth do crush their Wine;
> The Nectarene, and curious Peach,
> Into my hands themselves do reach;
> Stumbling on Melons, as I pass,
> Insnar'd with Flow'rs, I fall on Grass.
>
> Mean while the Mind, from pleasure less,
> Withdraws into its happiness:
> The Mind, that Ocean where each kind

Does streight its own resemblance find;
Yet it creates, transcending these,
Far other Worlds, and other Seas,
Annihilating all that 's made
To a green Thought in a green Shade.

Here at the Fountains sliding foot,
Or at some Fruit-trees mossy root,
Casting the Bodies Vest aside,
My Soul into the boughs does glide:
There like a Bird it sits, and sings,
Then whets, and combs its silver Wings;
And, till prepar'd for longer flight,
Waves in its Plumes the various Light.

He goes through three stages in these three verses, and I want mainly to look at the first one. Long ago I said that it refers to the Fall of Man, also that two verses in 'Upon Appleton House' refer to the Crucifixion, but Professor Legouis disagreed: and his Notes in the standard text of Marvell[2] are still saying 'Empson is wrong'. I think Legouis was killing the poetry in the interests of decorum; and you must certainly use this text òf Marvell's poetry, as it gives all kinds of information not available elsewhere, so I can claim that the question is not out of date. I had better first try to remove what may be a cause of misunderstanding; I certainly do not think Marvell wanted to say anything here about the Fall, or the Crucifixion, because he is concentrated upon describing his experiences with Nature; but he uses these two comparisons, among others, as a way to describe the experiences more clearly.

The repeated ME can be slurred over in reading aloud but had surely better be allowed its natural weight, and when this is done it is clear that Marvell feels he is being got at: 'Why are you picking on *me*?' The lushness of it all has been making him feel uneasy, and now the fruits are begging him to eat them, as if they were girls, and he would not like girls to be as forward as that anyway. He has an obscure feeling of guilt, or at least of flustered outrage; other people can sit in the garden without being badgered. So he closes his eyes, and imagines other places, which he is somehow stimulated to do; heaven perhaps, but where the other seas are we cannot guess. Then he can look at the garden again, and his soul, which is a quite solid object,

can fly out into the fruit-tree and be easy there. It is a gentle
sequence, in a short poem, but convincing; it seems carefully
observed. What he has described is a slight teasing by fairies,
very like those in *A Midsummer Night's Dream*; he does not
claim any more intimate aquaintance with them in his own
person, though he makes the Mower speak of them with con-
fidence. He and Fairfax evidently believed in them in principle;
this becomes clear in his grossest poem of flattery to Fairfax,
'Bilborough Hill', where he says that the trees on this hill are
proud of their legal owner because of his successes in the world
of men; that seems to us beneath the dignity of a spirit, though I
suppose a classical poet could say it. But this poem adds '"Tis
credible', in brackets, as though nudging Fairfax, and saying
'Remember your Cornelius Agrippa, please'. It would ring very
false if he only meant: 'poets under Augustus were allowed to
use this belief for flattery, because their barbarous ancestors
had really believed it'. Also the actual doctrine of the Fall in
Hermes Trismegistus, which would be familiar to Fairfax, might
well occur to him in reading 'The Garden'. It says that soon
after the creation Man fell in love with Nature, because of her
beauty, and she naturally loved him back, but this was an
unfortunate entanglement for Man, because Nature was low-
class and he was booked for a grand connection in heaven; so
they always need to be separated; but still, the affair does them
both credit, in a way. The expensive fruits in 'The Garden'
belong to the same world of graceful sentiment; they are
inquisitive about Marvell, as young calves would be.

Professor Legouis in his Notes gives a quotation from
another critic:

'Stumbling', 'Insnar'd', and 'fall' would normally image sin to the
Puritan in Marvell, but here it is only on *Melons* that he stumbles, only
by *Flow'rs* that he is insnar'd, only on *Grass* that he falls. Thus by
contrasting the normal sin associations of these words with his safe
helplessness now, he presents the occasion as amiably ludicrous.

Legouis comments: 'This is making sense of Empson's sensing
"the Fall" here.' But it makes the poem complacent and foot-
ling; we should not want to have Marvell rolling on his back like
a spaniel, saying to Nature 'Oh mummy, please tickle my
tummy'; if he is having a vision of Nature, even a small one, he

needs to treat her with decent awe. My view does at least let him
rise to the height of being disconcerted and irritated.

— In the Latin version of the poem he goes much further, and
—expresses a positive fear as well as reverence. He expects an
English garden to be fairly small, whereas his Latin one might
be the park of a Roman Emperor, so the Latin poem 'Hortus'
overlaps the woodland of 'Upon Appleton House'. Desire is
admitted to be a source of pain, and even the gods rejoice at
being free from its fevers when they discover that they can love
vegetables; and yet Jupiter falls madly, suicidally in love with
an aged oak-tree, and Juno has never been in such despair. No
doubt this is meant to be funny, but 'Hortus' does not suggest
that the poet is sexless, as 'The Garden' does; indeed, he yearns
for a purer life. (Perhaps Lady Fairfax did not read Latin so
freely as her husband.) There is just one sentence about the
presence of Nature. He has described himself as wandering far
away into the still darkness of the garden; he takes no delight, he
says, in herds of men, the din of the circus, or the bellowing of
the market-place:

> sed me Penetralia veris,
> Horroresque trahunt muti, et Consortia sola.

A Commentary on 'The Garden' translates this as: 'Spring's
inner chambers and numinous silences draw me, and that solitary communion', which is literal but takes effect as hushing up.
Here is our English word horror, only different because the idea
of 'bristly' comes in. It would be fair to translate: 'They drag me
to them, the secret places of the spring-time, and the hair-
raising silences when alone with the Alone.' It may be objected
that 'alone with the Alone' belongs to Christian mysticism, but
the phrase itself is not specific, and whatever spirit Marvell met
in this wood it was not a companionable one.

Apart from this one profound line the Latin poem cannot be
called better than the English, as that has all the philosophical
part about the relations of mind and matter. A feeling of wonder
about this old question, and probably some recall of recent
controversy about it (Pomponazzi and the Mortalist heresy, for
instance), can be relied upon to make the presence of the spirits
more credible. I had puzzled about the meaning of less in
'Meanwhile the mind, from pleasure less, Withdraws into its

happiness', and Legouis said that this was merely the sentence of Aristotle, that the pleasures of the mind are greater than those of the senses. But he was thinking in French; in English an adjective is only put after its noun to make some point. (J. B. Leishman agreed with Legouis because he considered Marvell a slovenly poet who would do anything for a rhyme.) I think Kermode got the sensible answer, taking *from pleasure less* to mean 'because the mind takes less pleasure in the garden than the senses do'; but maybe the poet as a whole took less pleasure in it when the fruits became so pressing and forward. Then Legouis' Note insists that *curious* means 'made with art', and I agree that heat was used in growing the peaches ('Upon Appleton House', l. 341), but it may just as suitably mean 'desirous of knowing what one has no right to know' (5c in the *Oxford English Dictionary*). I was blamed for dragging in the idea that the mind is like a mirror, forming images of whatever comes before it; but this is just the commonplace view which we cannot escape, however much we prefer to regard the mind as like the sea, with its own sea-lions and sea-horses. Aristotle is thoroughly snubbed in the next verse, when the poet's soul becomes a solid object, playing in the tree. The question here is whether there can be anything in the mind which was not first in the senses; but it is not prominent in the poem as a whole.

Legouis has a splendid sentence about the major question:

In neo-Classical poetry nothing will remain of mythology but a *caput mortuum*, an inert phraseology, but with Marvell the fiery liquor that intoxicated the poets of the Renaissance has not yet entirely evaporated.

Excellent, but what can it mean, when translated out of High Mandarin, except that Marvell was still able to believe in fairies? Modern Eng. Lit. is extremely shy of making this admission about any serious author, but it was not considered so ludicrous then; from as early as 1590, at least ten of the Cambridge colleges, including Marvell's own, had the *De Occulta Philosophia* of Cornelius Agrippa in their libraries: and this tells you how to call up nymphs in water-meadows. Instead, Legouis produces a theory that Marvell had communion with real vegetables, not with 'allegories'; implying that all Middle Spirits are only allegories, and I suppose also that nobody ever really believed in Venus or Jupiter. But the phrase 'into my hands themselves do reach' labours to insist that these peaches are behaving in a very unvegetable manner. You cannot have much conversation with a creature while you are eating it, and when Marvell does report communion with Nature it is of a more remote and eerie kind.

Having thus removed the interest from the poem, Legouis points out that it is dull; and he blames the dullness upon the flippancy and triviality of the poet, who ends it by going back to his first jokes. But it is part of the structure, as well as being realistic, for the poet to emerge from his ecstasy and confess that he will himself soon be wishing for a return to the world; still more to remind himself that this garden, in its pious way, is a highly artificial one, a luxury of the grandee who won the Civil War. The floral imitation of a clock, for that matter, may be contrasting itself to a vista of historical time.

There is another case, even more impressive, I think, in 'Upon Appleton House'; and here again my view is denounced in the current Oxford text, so I am not grubbing up a forgotten controversy. Marvell has been following the agricultural year and arrived at the autumn, when the meadows around the river are flooded, and he retires to the woods; he remains there for quite a number of verses, emerging when the floods go down. He has become a kind of magician there, covered with the falling leaves:

> Under this *antick Cope* I move
> Like some great *Prelate of the Grove*.

He becomes free from anxiety.

> How safe, methinks, and strong, behind
> These Trees have I incamp'd my Mind;
> Where Beauty, aiming at the Heart,
> Bends in some Tree its useless Dart;
> And where the World no certain Shot
> Can make, or me it toucheth not.
> But I on it securely play,
> And gaul its Horsemen all the Day.

All the more, he becomes overtaken by terror at the thought of returning to the world, as surely he will have to do; unless the wood itself holds him by force, and he tells it to use the instruments of the crucifixion:

> Bind me ye *Woodbines* in your 'twines,
> Curle me about ye gladding *Vines*,
> And Oh so close your Circles lace,
> That I may never leave this Place:
> But, lest your Fetters prove too weak,
> Ere I your Silken Bondage break,
> Do you, *O Brambles*, chain me too,
> And courteous *Briars* nail me through.

No one has denied that *binding, fettering*, and *nailing through* fit the crucifixion: and I never thought this his only parallel. In the next verse he suggests using the penalty devised for pirates, who were staked down on the foreshore to drown slowly as the tide came up:

> Here in the Morning tye my Chain,
> Where the two Woods have made a Lane;
> While, like a *Guard* on either side,
> The Trees before their *Lord* divide;
> This, like a long and equal Thread,
> Betwixt two *Labyrinths* does lead.
> But, where the Floods did lately drown,
> There at the Ev'ning stake me down.

Legouis says that Marvell is not 'masochistic', but I had never supposed any disease. He does call the briars *courteous*, but pleading with the tormentor in this way was an extra source of pathos, familiar in the theatre. There is evidently an emotional pressure behind the passage, and it comes where the poem as a whole needs to reach a climax, before he expresses his final reverence for his pupil Maria. Here again (in his *Andrew Marvell*), after removing the crisis from the poem, Legouis complains that it is formless and trivial.

I grant that if the poet is just a professional tutor, looking forward to more such jobs after this one is over, the emotional pressure seems uncalled-for. But he had just been rescued from making a fool of himself in London, and would soon have to go back and make a position there; surely an attack of stage fright is only to his credit—not to have felt any would make him almost too unpunctureable. And the poem is written for the eye of

Fairfax, who understood very well how *the world* might *shoot* at him. The danger from *beauty, aiming at the heart* might be understood by anyone; after refusing to settle in the firm he could not afford a marriage good enough for his sisters to approve, and surely an employee of the Puritan Government could not risk an illicit affair. To talk as if he had nothing to worry about is merely blinkered.

There is nothing so far to excite a populist sentiment; indeed, admiring the country estate might put him in favour of the landed gentry. The wise thoughts of the General would, of course, be heard with attention, but a sudden and permanent conversion is likely to have a more emotional cause. I think he fell in love with the Mower. The tutor at the great house would be socially isolated; he would sometimes meet young ladies on their visits, but their mothers had told them never to look at a man owning less than a thousand acres—you could see it in every eye. Many readers of his love-poetry feel that he has an uneasy relation to the girls addressed; he is intensely interested, readily fascinated, but he does not seem to like them much. And he could not have easy relations with his inferiors either. It does him credit, I think, to have raised himself above this dismal situation by regarding a mower with (necessarily distant) yearning. At the hay-making in 'Upon Appleton House', indeed, he says that

> every Mowers wholesome Heat
> Smells like an *Alexanders sweat*,

but this seems to be a loose generalization; only one of them gets the full treatment in 'Damon the Mower';

> I am the Mower *Damon*, known
> Through all the Meadows I have mown.
> On me the Morn her dew distills
> Before her darling Daffadils.
> And, if at Noon my toil me heat,
> The Sun himself licks off my Sweat.
> While, going home, the Ev'ning sweet
> In cowslip-water bathes my feet.

Damon keeps saying he is in despair for love of a woman, and this allows love to be talked about, but he would not have accepted the situation so passively. It is the poet who is in love with Damon; Freud calls the device 'displacement', when interpreting dreams. They are exquisite poems, and much better when this obvious point is admitted. The only classical use of the name Thestylis comes in the second eclogue of Virgil, which gives a straightforward treatment of the real situation, and it is recalled here for a woman who brings the haymakers their dinner; Marvell was not hiding his source with any care. So the theme was a convention, you may answer; but which parts of it are conventional? I do not know that any other poet has praised the smell of a farm hand.

This must have occurred to a number of people who kept tactfully silent about it, but it has a relevance; it fits his secret marriage to his housekeeper, in later life. An article by F. Tupper[3] in 1938 is commonly thought to disprove the marriage, but this is an obvious hush-up and ought not to have succeeded for so long. (I have been to the Record Office to make sure, and hope to print the results soon.) According to the statement of his widow, which was never confuted, he married her in the Liberty of the Minories, where the records were kept specially guarded for an eventual announcement; probably he intended to announce it when he retired. He hid it because he was afraid of his sisters, who would be indignant at such a marriage and might make mischief; they succeeded in hushing it up after his death, which came entirely unexpectedly.

The literary styles of a Cavalier poet and a Puritan controversialist are so very different that it is not clear what Marvell would consider permitted. But we need not doubt that Mrs. Palmer was his mistress before they married, because he (practically) told the Hull Corporation so. He hardly ever makes a personal remark to them, but the following (9 February 1667) is written just after the Plague and the Fire, and when the Dutch are winning the war. Marvell feels he has to warn them against fires in Hull:

We haue had so much of them here in the South that it makes me almost superstitious ... But Gods providence in such cases is well pleas'd to be frustrated by humane industry but much more his mercyes are always propitious to our repentance.

The superstitious view would be that God was punishing the wicked King and his debauched courtiers, and some hurried angel might mistake Marvell for a debauched courtier unless he married Mrs. Palmer. He married about three months after writing this letter; and since there was a secret marriage every day at the Little Minories, presumably one would have had to book ahead. In *The Rehearsal Transpros'd*, when he was rebuking the Jesuitical laxity of Parker, he says that all kinds of evil, even war, come

most of all from the Corruption of Manners, and alwayes fatal Debauchery. It exhausts the Estates of private persons, and makes them fit for nothing but the High-way, or an Army.[4]

Clearly this comes from the heart, but it could hardly apply to his relations with his housekeeper, even before they were married, as she cost him nothing so far as we learn. Several times, in *The Rehearsal Transpros'd* and other prose writings, he remarks that a celibate clergy are patently either hypocrites or living unnaturally; since he was keeping his own marriage hidden, he must have expected his readers to think some such arrangement normal.

Six pamphlets attacked the First Part of *The Rehearsal Transpros'd* and most of them accused the author of both sodomy and impotence. Marvell laughs at them for a moment in the Second Part, but makes no reply; and yet he must have known he would be thought to be recalling these accusations when he made an apparent confession to Parker:

For mine own part I have, I confess, some reason, perhaps particular to my self, to be diffident of mine own *Moral Accomplishments*, & therefore may be the more inclinable to think I have a necessity of some extraordinary assistance to sway the weakness of my belief, and to strengthen me in good duties. If you be stronger I am glad of it; and let every man after he has read and consider'd what we have of it in the Scripture, and what even in our Common Prayer book, take what course and opinion he thinks the safest.[5]

Because of the variety of men, their consciences need more liberty than the authoritarian Parker assumes—that is all he needs to say, but he gives it a great air of spiritual depth. Commentators who notice the accusations at all generally say that the accusers found they could not catch him out in casual relations with women, and felt that was sinister enough in itself. I thought the explanation likely till I found this 'confession'; as a rule, if a man says he is unique, even if only for a tease, he really does think he is a bit special. Marvell had now been five years married, and maybe the private joke is merely that his wife is the 'extraordinary assistance'; but probably he could have enlarged on that. It was a time when the claims of ladies were felt to be severe; compare the Cleopatra of Shakespeare with Dryden's lady in *All for Love*, who obviously could not have ruled Egypt because she could not leave her drawing-room. Even King Charles himself, who could put up with ladies better than anyone, sometimes needed the fresh air of Nell Gwyn. Probably Marvell had had some cause to suspect himself of impotence, and had been relieved to find that he was quite all right with Mrs. Palmer—it was only *ladies* who froze him up. This at least would give the sentence as much point as it seems to demand.

I submit that he was putting on an act in Restoration London, pretending to be poor and low-class, because that was the best means of mobilizing votes on his side; not at all a martyrdom, because it also suited his feelings, but he is decidedly upper-class when writing to Yorkshire. His enemy Parker said at the time that Marvell was obviously bred up among boatswains and cabinboys (presumably he knew that Marvell had been in the shipping trade); and in later life, when he could invent more freely, though subject to check by other old men, he said there were a whole set of poverty-struck M.P.s like Marvell:

But these fellows could never carry one point in the House, for they were always treated with the utmost scorn and contempt . . . . As soon as one of them opened his mouth he was hissed, and as often as our poet spoke, he was cudgelled for it.[6]

Marvell does seem to have been a bad speaker in the House, unless the few records are malignant, but anyhow his main work was done in committee. Compare now what Sir Henry Thompson writes to Marvell, in December, 1675. Sir Henry is a pattern of advancement through the Hull wine trade. After being Lord Mayor of York, he bought a country house and became the first Thompson of Escrick Park, a long line; also he is, at the time of writing, the head of the Thompson family in Hull:

I pay you my sincere thanks for your protection & repeated favors & I humbly beseech you to believe yt with the best understanding I have I will ever honour you in the acknowledging of them.[7]

Almost at once he is teasing Marvell about a rich old Non-comformist woman, recently become a widow, whom Marvell had better marry; they are on easy terms; it seems that Marvell was trying, not very hard, to clear up some obstacle against his becoming M.P. for York. I suggest that the reason for this one extravagantly polite sentence is that the Thompson family firm, still based on Hull, is among those clubbing together to provide a salary for Marvell; he wants to show, briefly but firmly, that he accepts Marvell as an equal not a hired man. At any rate it is startlingly different from the picture of him in London.

We can name at least four firms who would be contributing to this allowance, and we should realize that they thought it proper. The Corporation only paid a small dole while Parliament was sitting, and usually only a rich old spokesman would get the job, but if a skilled whole-time expert were needed he must of course get a salary. It is not till 1726 that we hear of Marvell starving in a garret and daffing aside the foppish lords from the Court who offer him a fortune. The big men of Hull, at the time, really did think Marvell an honest man, but they would not usually have taken the risk of putting a man's honesty under so heavy a strain. The wicked Farrington, after Marvell was dead, said that he never had any money except what he got by cadging; and well might Farrington mouth these words, if he had stolen the entire hoard. His remark serves to make clear that Marvell looks better as a salaried man than as a moral hero. And I think a decisive piece of evidence can be found in his housing arrangements. His letters north are headed or ended 'Westminster' or 'Covent Garden' or 'Highgate', taking for granted that his full address in each district is known to the correspondent. He uses all of them even during the last year of his life, while he is actually living at his secret hide-out for Hull bankrupts in the sanctuary of St. Giles. Now, if a man lives and dresses in a very modest way, and has modest lodgings in London—but three or four modest lodgings, that means he is trying to hide his riches. Probably Marvell was saving to be able to retire, as he urges his nephew to do that, but there is no reason to doubt that he and his wife were living comfortably.

'Clarendon's House-Warming', the first of the satires, was written in July or late June 1667, about two months after the wedding. It was another unreasonable result of the series of disasters, and again a fortunate one, as it helped to set Clarendon free to complete his history. The poem is not ascribed to Marvell before 1726, and the first question is: 'How could he possibly have written so badly?' It is more or less in anapaests, a rhythm used mainly for songs, and has verses, as a song does; a number of similar poems were written in the next ten years, one of which says on the title-page that it is a song ('To the tune *Which Nobody can Deny*'), so presumably they all were. I do not know of anyone who has discussed the scansion except Legouis, who positively likes it; one should acknowledge here, he says,

... the presence of the Old, or at least the Middle, English accentual verse. ... Marvell ... showed the promise it held. He thus fought the ankylosis that threatened the poetry of his age, his own included, owing to its excessive submission to syllabic rules.[8]

One need not deny that bad verse often uses the native rhythms of colloquial English, and thus makes good prose. This has happened, for instance, in the line:

To buy a king is not so wise as to sell.

But surely it is not 'accentual'. One cannot even say where the accents go. It might be called 'syllabic'; the man has counted eleven syllables, so that the words could fit the notes. Legouis does quote a line with a lot of short syllables, but very few are like that; maybe the author would complain that he had been misreported, or 'hadn't quite finished'. Most of the time we hear a pathetic struggle to hammer out anapaests, as in the lines from 'The Statue at Charing Cross':

The TROjan horse, THO' not of BRASS but of WOOD,
Had within it an Army that burnt up the Town.

This galumphs, but is meant to scan. Surely it has nothing to do with Anglo-Saxon poetry. On the other hand there are some very good verses in 'Clarendon's House-Warming' which seem clearly by Marvell; this of course is why the poem was ascribed to him later. If you number the verses and mark the ones likely to be Marvell's, the solution leaps to the eye. We are confronted by communal authorship, which enthusiasts for the ballad have ascribed to the primeval dancing horde: the ultimate sacrifice of a poet to democracy. One of the merits of it was to make the contributors feel safe, though brave, because no one of them had written the poem.

There are ten badly scanned verses, then two good verses by Marvell, evidently prepared beforehand; he has five guests, and has put himself at the end of the line. Then there is one loose and jovial verse by Marvell; they have given him an encore. This verse is about two jackals of Clarendon who recently came into the House drunk together, which not many people would know about; probably the five guests are M.P.s. Then ten more bad verses, then two good ones by Marvell. These are rather too literary, though very like Marvell; he does not get an encore here. Probably the second time round was an unexpected mark of success, and he had had to invent his contribution while waiting his turn. Then came three final verses about what they hope to do to Clarendon when Parliament meets, on 25 July; the main points here would be arranged at the start, because knowing the end always gives a comforting suggestion that things are in hand. They would meet in an upstairs room at a pub, as this was not treason, only politics, and a fiddler would be in attendance, to play the well-known tune that would be repeated for each verse. The drawer was probably responsible for recording the text, and no doubt he sometimes got a bit muddled. Marvell puts himself at the end because he must not outshine his guests; they must feel that making up verse is an easy thing to do. The poem is a series of random jeers and accusations against Clarendon, which is a likely result from the method. Having come so far, I realized that Marvell would have had to get his guests started, with a firm statement of the theme; a polite ducking away would not be enough. And indeed I had been mistaken about the first two verses; they are very strong and competent; but the first line of the poem is in flat prose, and the next two lines stumble on purpose. He would write them himself beforehand and give them to his stooge, who sat next to him; they state the theme extremely strongly. One must recall that Apollo is the god of plague (he starts the *Iliad* by sending a plague), and *brume* need only mean winter.

When Clarindon had discern'd beforehand,
  (As the Cause can eas'ly foretel the Effect)
At once three Deluges threatning our land;
  'Twas the season he thought to turn Architect.

Us *Mars*, and *Apollo*, and *Vulcan* consume;
  While he the betrayer of *England* and *Flander*,
Like the Kingfisher chuseth to build in the Broom
  And nestles in flames like the Salamander.

None of the other M.P.s can work up anything near the lunacy of Marvell on the topic; they do not even mention that Clarendon had caused the Plague (presumably by black magic). The first line, I submit, must be intentionally prose; the 'simpsonian' rhyme-word, off the beat, ends it with a complete deflation. It is stressed 'When ... Clar ... Cern ... Fore'; how it is sung I do not know, but modern reciters have found that one can intone rather against than with a background of music. When Marvell comes on in person he is entirely in control of the metre, and accuses Clarendon of quite possible things such as commandeering materials for his palace. Someone once said that the 'Ancient Mariner' feels as if the English language was invented for the one purpose of writing this poem, and there is a verse here which has something of the same power:

His Wood would come in at the easier rate,
  So long as the Yards had a Deal or a Spar:
His Friends in the Navy would not be ingrate,
  To grudge him some Timber who fram'd them the War.

Loony of course, but really very good poetry. Legouis remarks contentedly that '27 only out of 112 lines consist of anapaests' and it looks as if these are the seven quatrains contributed by Marvell, omitting the first line. If Legouis got so far, it seems a pity that he felt no further curiosity.

    Clarendon was impeached in November, and after his fall no song against him was likely to be revived; so we may hope that the 'House-Warming' gives the original order of verses. As a rule, songs against the King would go on having new verses added. Also Marvell would not often join in communal composition; it was enough if he could set a fashion so that other people would do it. However, he would often be asked to improve such a poem, and evidently concentrated on getting more of a bang at the end; 'The Statue at Charing Cross' is an example, not at all consecutive, very uneven in capacity for scansion, and never feeling like Marvell till the last verse. (The statue is of Charles I.)

> So the Statue will up after all this delay,
> But to turn the face to Whitehall you must Shun;
> Tho of Brass, yet with grief it would melt him away,
> To behold every day such a Court, such a son.

The second line turns back to iambics for dramatic effect, and perhaps to keep in touch with the rhythmic confusion of the rest of the poem. Margoliouth reports very little ascription of it to Marvell, and this one verse is surely the only reason for giving it to him. 'The Statue in Stocks-Market' is a consecutive joke or argumentative reflection, pretty certainly by one author, but the last two verses are again notably better than the rest. The author may have asked Marvell to cocker it up, or he might have been able to imitate Marvell.

'The Kings Vowes', I would say, is the only poem other than the 'House-Warming' which was written partly by Marvell in communal composition, taking turns round a table; and here the conditions are set by the first lines, so that writing the poem would be like taking part in a game. The date is 1670. This time there are only three guests, and they scan quite well; perhaps they are business men not M.P.s. The order is not perfect, but the Notes give evidence that one verse was added a year later, also strong evidence that the poem went on being sung, so a few changes of order are likely. The guests are rather brutal about the King, regarding him with contempt and anger; but Marvell finds him harmless and ridiculous, and pathetically bothered by his self-made problems. The distinction once noticed is very clear-cut, I think; and if you take the Marvell verses alone, the poem feels soft; so here for once the method positively makes the poem better.

Here are the parts of the first draft which I believe to be Marvell's:

> When the Plate was at pawne, and the fob att low Ebb,
> And the Spider might weave in our Stomack its web;
>> Our Pockets as empty as braine;
>> Then Charles without acre

Made these Vowes to his Maker—
If ere I see England again,

1

I will have a Religion then all of my owne,
Where Papist from Protestant shall not be knowne;
But if it grow troublesome, I will have none.

7

I will have a fine Son in makeing tho marrd,
If not o're a Kingdome, to raigne ore my Guard;
And Successor be, if not to me, to Gerrard.

11

But what ever it cost I will have a fine Whore,
As bold as Alce Pierce and as faire as Jane Shore;
And when I am weary of her, I'le have more.

15

I will have a fine Tunick a Sash and a Vest,
Tho' not rule like the Turk yet I will be so drest,
And who knowes but the Mode may soon bring in the rest?

Margoliouth lets drop that he would be pleased to relieve Marvell of this poem, but has not got enough evidence. I do not know why he should feel so; the poem is quite free from the self-deluding hatred of the attack on Clarendon. Up to this date, but not afterward, Marvell believed that some good use might be made of Charles, who at least was against religious persecution, and seemed otherwise unaggressive; laughing at him was a useful source of solidarity among anti-royalists, but had best be treated as fun. Lord Gerrard actually had commanded the King's Guard till the recent appointment of Monmouth; Marvell probably backed Monmouth as the next king, and thought it pathetic for Charles to say, with rueful delicacy, that at least he can give the boy a job around the house. Verse 11 has the confident voice of a spoiled child, but a scrupulous child who has searched English history for precedents. The scheme of verse 15, to use Turkish dress as a psychological preparation for absolute rule, admits that he is a plotter but makes him a fatuous one. I should add that one of the other verses calls

Buckingham the King's pimp, and it has been objected that Marvell would never have written a poem which said that—he always did his best for Buckingham, who had married the Maria of 'Appleton House'. No indeed, but Marvell could not censor the jokes made by others; this point is an argument for communal authorship. In the same way, he praises Buckingham in one of the verses he wrote for the 'House-Warming', and no one else would have done it, in such a poem.

K. H. D. Haley, in *William of Orange and the English Opposition* (1953), describes a struggle during the years 1672–4 to get a majority in Parliament against war with the Dutch; many M.P.s came to suspect that the King was taking French money to help the Papist cause, and that to let French Papists overrun Holland would be too dangerous. It is a pleasure to learn that Marvell (according to the King's spies) was the only M.P. with a code name for the correspondence with William of Orange; but it still seems possible that the busy activity of propaganda was not what brought about the decision—this came when the future James II announced that he was a Papist. In any case, Marvell was henceforward sternly disillusioned with Charles. In 1675, during a campaign to impeach the Prime Minister, Danby, he picked up a copy of 'The Kings Vowes', now five years old, and it seemed to him much too soft: he wrote some poetry at the foot of the page, without noticing that his new solemn rhythm would not fit the tune:

> Some one I will advance from mean descent,
> So high that he shall brave the Parliament,
> And all their bills for publick good prevent.

> And I will take his part to that degree
> That all his dareing crimes, what ere they be,
> Under my hand and Seal shall have Indemnity.

> I wholly will abandon State affaires,
> And pass my Time with Parrasites and Players,
> And Visit Nell when I shold be att Prayers.

Margoliouth very rightly prints this in his text, giving lower down the page the altered version in the *State Poems*, made casually by someone else for singing—'And I will assert him to such a Degree, That all his foul Treasons tho' daring and high' and so on. But his comment is: 'The text at the end of M16 [the manuscript he accepts] is rather lame.' If Margoliouth was editing a sonnet sequence, and one of the sonnets turned out to be a limerick, would he say that the text was rather lame? These lines are majestic. And surely, it is only the leader of a communal song who would be treated so seriously as a contributor, and yet with such indifference as a poet, that his lines would be destroyed as poetry to fit them for the tune. The successive editors are queerly unable to realize what is happening.

This theory about the songs is useful if it lets us pick out and appreciate the bits by Marvell, but does not go very deep. The last poem by Marvell is 'A Dialogue between the Two Horses' (1675), not a song though in anapaests and, I think, clearly all his own. This provides an opportunity to reconsider the contempt usually expressed for the Satires. They are not about Nature, and hardly even draw metaphors from Nature, therefore, we are told, they are prosy; and they are partisan, making no attempt to see both sides of a question, so they have no vision. Margoliouth even says that a flat analogy from bees in 'The Loyall Scot' is 'the last example we have of his poetry properly so called', but this mysterious propriety needs to be examined. It is true that the Satires do not expect their public to believe in fairies, who were no longer popular, but this limitation can be got round. The earlier poems, 'To His Coy Mistress' and 'The Coronet' for example, do not regularly and obviously sit on the fence; and, if they do it in a subtle and secondary way, perhaps the 'Dialogue' does too. The horses are the mounts of the two statues of the kings who are so often discussed in these poems, and they represent public opinion, which is sick of the Stuarts, or at least the purpose of the poem is to make it so. But they are also very like horses; as they are herd animals, they discover from being together what they both feel, and they have none of the duty of courage natural to a flesh-eater or a military aristocrat, though they are strong when they are roused. Woolchurch and Charing are the stations of the two horses, but both they and their riders move freely at night. Charing, the steed of Old Charles, takes longer to warm up. The rhythm is highly dramatic; in the following quotation there are long pauses, for example, after 'Cromwell' and before 'a Tyrant's', and 'I am' gets two heavy stresses:

whereas the previous break-through of Woolchurch runs like a
spate:

    W. Truth's as Bold as a Lyon, I am not afraid;
        I'le prove every tittle of what I have said.
        Our riders are absent; who is't that can hear?
        Letts be true to ourselves; whom then need wee fear? . . .
    Ch. De Witt and Cromwell had each a brave soul.
    W. I freely declare it, I am for old Noll.
    Ch. Tho' his Government did a Tyrants resemble,
        Hee made England great and it's enemies tremble.

Woolchurch is wonderfully like a horse; you can hear him
squeal. Surely it was very absurd of Legouis to say that this
versification is exactly like the incompetence of 'The Statute at
Charing Cross', and that both are part of a revival of Anglo-
Saxon poetry?

    Coming now to magic, of course you are not meant to believe
in the talking statues of horses; they are political cartoons. But
they are intended to work on you like magic; the author says so
very clearly at the beginning and end. Talking horses come even
in the Bible as well as the classics, he says, and of course a
prophecy from statues of horses will be even more reliable. In
fact, the more they are like horses the more they are the voice
of the people; and after making their final pronouncement ridiculous the author can turn round and agree with what they
say:

    Ch. But canst thou Divine when things shall be mended?
    W. When the Reign of the Line of the Stuarts is ended.
    Ch. Then, England, Rejoyce, thy Redemption draws nigh;
        Thy oppression togeather with Kingship shall dye.
    W. A Commonwealth a Common-wealth wee proclaim to the
        Naccion;
        The Gods have repented the Kings Restoration. . . .

Conclusion

But I should have told you, before the Jades parted,
Both Gallopt to Whitehall and there Horribly farted,
Which Monarchys downfall portended much more
Than all that the beasts had spoken before. . . .
Tho' Tyrants make Laws which they strictly proclaim
To conceal their own crimes and cover their shame,

Yet the beasts of the field or the stones in the wall
Will publish their faults and prophesy their fall.

I do not feel that there is any shortage of Natural Magic here.

NOTES

1. *Andrew Marvell*, ed. John Carey, Penguin Critical Anthologies, (1969), pp. 22–3.
2. *The Poems and Letters of Andrew Marvell*, 3rd edn., rev. P. Legouis and E. E. Duncan-Jones, 2 vols (Oxford, 1971).
3. F. S. Tupper, 'Mary Palmer, alias Mrs Marvell', PMLA, 53, 1938.
4. *The Rehearsal Transpros'd*, ed. D. I. B. Smith (Oxford, 1971), p. 56.
5. Op. cit., 268.
6. Samuel Parker, *History of His Own Time* (1728), p. 216.
7. Margoliouth, II, p. 392.
8. P. Legouis, *Andrew Marvell: Poet, Puritan, Patriot*, 2nd edn. (Oxford, 1968), p. 188.

III

THE SHOOTING OF THE BEARS: POETRY AND POLITICS IN ANDREW MARVELL

by BARBARA EVERETT

OUTSIDE the universities, if a reading audience still exists there, Marvell is the author of one poem. 'To his Coy Mistress' is perhaps a surprising work to have kept alive the name of the reserved bachelor who wrote it. But this kind of mild surprise is frequent with Marvell. He is not at all an easy writer to see whole: the life and the reputation, the career and the work he left, have meant different things to different people. The man behind the lyrics is unusually elusive to us. Perhaps this is why Marvell has never really been a great poet to the general reader. For until about fifty years ago, the poems now regarded as some of our greatest lyrics were almost entirely neglected; and if Marvell is a great poet, then he is the only one we have who has stayed unread in this way for nearly two hundred years. Most great writers manage to survive, in one way or another. But Marvell did not—until half a century ago he emerged, rediscovered by poets and academics. He became what he remains, not the author of a single classic love poem, but something like the most admired of all 'critics' poets'. A decade or so ago, criticism began to take a new turn. The rediscovered poet had been the writer of the best lyrics. But Marvell in fact left behind him a much larger body of occasional work, most of it the outgrowth of his life in politics. When Marvell died, he was known—well known, and in some quarters much admired—as a public person, and the author of often combative and polemic literature. His lyrics stayed unpublished until several years after his death, and he seems rarely to have chosen to pass them around in manuscript—the usual custom of gentlemen of the period who did not wish for social reasons to publish their work. Marvell was known, instead, as the panegyrist of Cromwell and then the M.P. for Hull; the writer of brilliant satirical verses on the part of the 'Country' against the Court of Charles II, and of brave and successful prose defences of the Good Old Cause—in particular, of religious toleration. Criticism has begun to include in its appreciation some of the best of this large body of occasional writing, a good deal of which appeared anonymously in the first instance, thus raising lasting doubt as to its authorship. Even if it had not been anonymously published, the style of many of these verse satires, panegyrics, and commemorations of events, not to mention the works in prose, is different enough from that of the best lyrics to create real problems in discussing them. Despite these problems both of identification and of judgement, most of the major occasional poems—the salute to Cromwell on the First Anniversary of his Government, the elegy on his death, the satire called 'The Last Instructions to a Painter'—have all been studied recently with enthusiasm and interest.

This sharp rise of interest in the public poetry may well be an attempt, however little conscious, to come to terms with the strangeness that exists in Marvell's work, and in his career and reputation: to diminish the sense of fissure in it. A number of good critics have shown that a mind distinctly Marvellian is at work in the more authentic of the public poems.[1] But it is a thing that needs showing. Most ordinary, and—even now—most professional readers of Marvell are liable to be aware of the disjunctions in the work. The difference in kind and indeed in value between the best lyrics and the best occasional poems is enough to explain why Marvell has been systematized into a mythical chronology. There is no evidence for the dating of most of the best poems—that is to say, the lyrics; the occasional poems, almost by definition, are often written for a date. It is entirely customary, though the assumptions have not gone unchallenged, to take it that Marvell's lyrics are pre-Restoration, and that most of the public poetry is at least post-1650.[2] Marvell is assumed to have grown out of writing lyric poetry and into writing satire, a more mature even if a distinctly coarser style and vision. But this assumption is dangerous though deeply based. It ignores the possibility that a writer of Marvell's studied brilliance and variety might have written very variously at various points of his life, and was capable of writing in or out of fashion when he was writing—after all—for no one but himself. It remains possible that

Marvell wrote occasional poems and lyrics side by side throughout the whole of his writing life: and to assume otherwise may be to read into both kinds of poetic practice ideas about their different relation to truth and seriousness which are simply not justified. And the exact relation to truth of both 'private' and 'public' writing is a question which, I think, had some meaning for Marvell.

The sense of fragmentation in the poet's work is reflected in his peculiar career after death. For a while remembered as a distinctive public figure, he gradually lapsed into nearly two centuries of silence: before reviving, with immense acclaim, in our own time. Though this is a history rare among great poets, it is not rare among the lesser writers of Marvell's own period. Herrick waited years to publish his first volume; it came out in 1648 and met complete failure; he died without knowing success and moved into that 'great gap of time' which Marvell knew as well, until both began to be read again a little by poets in the early nineteenth century. The fate they both endured has a rhythm that can be recognized; it is part of the cultural history of the last four hundred years. By the 1680s writers of only two generations back had become the 'giant race before the Flood'. Most of the best minor poetry of the previous age, and even the shorter poems of several major figures, sank and almost drowned in the 'flood' which shaped the century. If we try to explain that great historic shift, then an aspect of what happened to Marvell may give a clue to it. For not all Marvell's work was lost—something survived. When the lyrics were published in 1681, they sank almost without trace. But the reputation of the public work survived. Marvell was remembered, not entirely accurately, as a kind of proto-Whig, a Protestant hero and a Republican poet: until the passing of time paradoxically destroyed what virtue the occasional nature of the work had seemed to hold. The poems that were lost first were those that were first recovered: the private poems.

It might be argued that all good verse is public, or public enough to communicate with good readers. But Renaissance poets probably thought instinctively of the 'private' and 'public' realms as clearly divided: as clearly divided as was the personal life from what Marvell called 'our Lady State'. On the other hand, it is true that if the poetry written at the turn of the

sixteenth century demands extreme respect, this is because of
the way in which private and public matters are fused within it.
The love poetry of Shakespeare, Donne, and Raleigh is heroic
in scale, import, and intensity. Private poetry of this quality
goes beyond a formal category; it sets an ethical standard. If,
fifty years ago, poets and academics rediscovered seventeenth-
century poetry, then it was probably private poetry they were
discovering, rather than merely experiencing a taste for the
Metaphysical; and what they were experiencing probably went
beyond questions of mere taste at all. Donne and Marvell 'came
back' because many intelligent individuals felt or thought they
felt a severance from the civilization that both created and
threatened them. Marvell rose into prominence, in the 1920s
and '30s, as the creator of an acutely private art; and to read his
brilliant, individual poems was perhaps like inheriting, at the
end of a throttling civilization, a small landed estate to retreat to
and to live in freely. If taste is turning now, as it seems to be,
towards the occasional verse, then this probably says more
about our own ever more publicly-orientated society—in many
ways a second Restoration period—than it does about Marvell's
poems.[3]

We perhaps now underrate the insistency—suggestive in
terms of his own feeling, even if not literally true—of Marvell's
own remark, in *The Rehearsal Transpros'd*, that 'I never had any,
not the remotest relation to publick matters' before 1657, when
he accepted a governmental appointment: reluctantly, so he
said. Whenever they were written, the virtues of Marvell's best
poems are those of a man who, from an unusual integrity and
toughness of character, refused—or found himself unable—to
abandon his privacy as a poet. A contrast might be made with
his great predecessor, from whom he learned so much: Ben
Jonson. Jonson's best work is high public art: but the private
personality behind it is simple in the extreme; hence the real
human limitations behind the poet's always beautifully used
rhetoric. Marvell's lyrics inherit, gratefully, that lucid exposit-
ory style which Jonson created and gave to the literature of his
time, but the result is scarcely confusable with the work of the
older poet. When Marvell actually brought Jonson in person
into one of his poems, making him speak from the underworld
in 'Tom May's Death', he invented for him—significantly—a

high resonance of rhetoric that was then conceivable as years out of date, and simply inutile in the real complex circumstances of modern political life: life in the 1650s. Marvell's own 'true' lyrics possess something like the Jonsonian lucidity—but they inform it, ironically, with a private personality that is wholly different in kind: self-mocking, subtle, and permanently reserved. It is this private character which gives to Marvell's verse its chief endowment (after its obvious literary skills): a strikingly original sensibility. When we open an anthology we recognize Marvell at once. And we do so, not so much by the sound of a voice, as by the quality of a whole mind, a mind whose recesses it is not easy to exhaust. In a way, of course, it would be foolish first to notice the poet's peculiar individuality, and then to think of this as characteristic of an age. But there is little doubt that certain periods help to form (or to destroy) the selfhood of the persons within them; and that the first half of the seventeenth century produced an extraordinary number of talented poets, the least of whom is characterized by the flavour of individuality. Marvell's remarkably original sensibility, the degree to which he existed as a 'private' man, has to be seen against the background of change and development in the whole world of the later Renaissance. The Tudors had left England with a sense of its own greatness, and possessed, if not of wealth, at least of the tastes and expectations of the rich. The England of the 1620s, '30s and '40s where Marvell grew up—and while the rest of Europe was beginning to be torn by war—was in consequence experiencing a form of highly cultivated self-realization. Post-Tudor England saw the discovery of the formal private life, the projection on to the forms of society itself of the impulses of civilized inwardness. In the seventeenth century England becomes a country of high-walled gardens and collectors' cabinets. Its gentlemen hang their houses with muffling silk and with silencing Turkey carpets; its ladies read romances and write letters. Its finest aristocrats withdraw from the capital and make of their estates a 'college in a purer air'. The King himself is an amateur and a collector, who seeks to keep not only his Court but even his country as his private property, and leaves behind him in the chaos of the 1650s—when Marvell's career really begins—what might have been the best art-gallery in Europe. After the Civil

Wars even the poor joined in, and began to level England, or so they hoped, towards a dreamed-of Fifth Monarchy of the mind.

One of Marvell's most distinguished scholars, Pierre Legouis, described his 'Bermudas' as a legend under crystal. Many of the best poems have something of this quality of enchanted self-enclosure; it is the source of their strength as well as of their charm. Marvell moved towards some of the devices of the self-consistent imagination discovered two hundred years later by the French Symbolists. Many of his poems have all Mallarmé's love of the small, the precious, and the innocent. But Marvell's mowers and glow-worms, children, flowers and fruit are, strictly speaking, collectors' pieces: cut, polished and set. His wonderfully subtle and disturbing 'The Mower against Gardens' makes of the collecting mind itself a kind of everlasting flower, or a coral preserved in the garden-cabinet of fallen time and space:

> The Pink grew then as double as his Mind;
> The nutriment did change the kind.

Those who celebrate Marvell primarily as a Nature poet are right to do so. But his landscapes are most frequently only moments of time in which the world's 'rarities' startlingly catch the light: like the dew-drop

> Dark beneath, but bright above

or like

> The hatching *Thrastles* shining Eye

that suddenly looks at us out of the lines of 'Appleton House'; or like that fruit of the Bermudas,

> the Orange bright,
> Like golden Lamps in a green Night.

Marvell's natural world exists to give back the profound shock of perception: a delighted-in limitation and circularity, which comes to the surface in the poet's fascination with eyes and tears—eyes rarely without their fruit of tears, tears reflecting like diamonds. The dew-drop, the thrush's eye and the lit-up orange tree are similarly so formal as to be almost in themselves Renaissance jewels, but jewels released into innocence by the poet's pervasive moral integrity: that tacit self-judgement and self-mockery which always destroys the garlands, opens up the galleries and dissolves the drop of dew, forbidding an over-valuing of what it has made.

If Marvell had been no more than a private poet in this sense, we should probably not be remembering the tercentenary of his death, but merely including him with that splendid gallery of Caroline connoisseurs who gave the age its elegance—a Lovelace who survived, a more eccentric Herrick. But Marvell is better than this, and bigger too. In the 'Horatian Ode' he wrote what may be the greatest political poem in English, a poem that stands like a landmark at the centre of the age: grave, weighty, and unshakeably judicious. But even in the poems that make no claims to public statement Marvell is much more than an artist in rarities. 'To his Coy Mistress' has a largeness, a substance, reflected in though not explained by the grandeur of all its dismissed fantasies—its Ganges and its rubies, its empires and its slow-growing love. It is this sense of largeness of scale in the best poems that suggests, perhaps, the chief critical problem of Marvell's work. The lyrics commit themselves willingly to the small, but they are not small poems. Great images inhabit them without any of that strain, that distortion or even perversity which might go with their use in Augustan verse. Moreover, if we ask how a poet so elusive, so drily content with the minor forms of the age, could leave behind him—unpublished—these great lyrics, it does not help to call in some concept of the 'great personality', as we might in the case of a Donne, a Milton, or even a Dryden. For, though both the writing and the career suggest that Marvell had a strong character, he does not appear to have had a personality at all, whether great or small. The public Marvell, the man whom the age saw, seems to be a blank. He rarely spoke in Parliament; Clarendon does not mention him. The handwriting in a letter to his constituency that survives in the British Museum is startlingly simple and regular, like the hand of a nineteenth-century office clerk; and this man of extraordinarily original sensibility seems to have maintained in his address to the world in general, to his acquaintances as to his constituency, just such an impersonal, flavourless rectitude. One of the most idio-syncratic poets in existence, called by Burnet 'the liveliest droll of the day'; a man who—so Aubrey suggests—loved his friends though he had no 'general acquaintance', Marvell also had no personality, at least in the public form which is an offshoot of egoism. This may be why he left behind him a handful of brilliant lyrics in all the manners of the time, but no artistic canon—no developing and datable body of work that preserves the laws of the psyche that produced it. This is also why, perhaps, even the very best of the occasional work, like the late satire 'The Last Instructions to a Painter', written in buoyant, brisk, and beautiful Restoration couplets, cannot compare in merit to the best satires of Dryden and Pope: whose attacking, far more egoistic energies subsume the minutiae of their time into a largely unjust but vital artistic harmony. Despite all his rhetorical skills, Marvell's very virtues—his essentially private decency and integrity, his strong loyalties, his amused attentive interest in the world around him—all the time seem to have prevented him from ever being an outstanding political poet: the crude mere 'occasion' dominates and disintegrates that patient artistic consciousness observing it. 'The Last Instructions' tells us something, and tells it brilliantly, about what it was like to live in the England of Charles II; it is still pleasurable and interesting to read, up to a point; but it is not a very good poem by Andrew Marvell.

The relative weakness of the occasional verse reflects the more credit on the man who tried to write it—who was not content to remain merely a private poet. And thereby it throws some light on the peculiar strength of the best lyrics. For the self-enclosure of Marvell's poems is not in fact as great as it seems to be, or as it drily advertises itself to be. The difference in scale between Marvell and, say, Herrick—good as Herrick is—might be summarized as the greater *openness* of a Marvell lyric. It contains more of life; of the world; of its time; it matches the superior and secure finesse of its forms with a superior freedom in the elusion of its forms. But a poem by Marvell will be exceedingly difficult to relate directly to the life of his time. Many attempts have been made to hear the noise of the Civil Wars in the cadences of the lyrics, but such attempts seem often to go counter to the poems, instead of with them. The openness of these poems is not easy to define. In part, this remarkably beautiful 'cabinet' poetry goes beyond the

standards it seems to set itself by virtue of the continual presence within it of irony; that highly intelligent irony which we
hear everywhere in the lyrics without ever finding it easy to
locate it convincingly. It may work as no more than a surprising
absence of insistence, rare in an age of dogmatism: a sceptical
'Convince me then that this is true', an 'It is to be supposed they
grieve'. Or it may take the form of a love of anti-climax, like the
'Let's in' that suddenly ends 'Appleton House', making of the
whole rambling, ambitious work not so much a poem as a stroll
around the garden, while the evening light fades. Such anti-
climax works perpetually in small ways too, as in Marvell's
pleasure in closing a forcible opening stanza concerning the
'forward youth' in war, with the derisive, difficult rhyme-word
languishing. This irony may relate more directly outwards, as in
the case of Marvell's curious titles. A private poem will be by its
'public' title mockingly associated with the world at large, as
though overheard. Thus, 'To his Coy Mistress': which is *not*, in
fact, a seduction poem, but something much lonelier; it tells,
not woos, and what it tells is not encouraging. 'The Definition
of Love' is *not* a definition, or not of love; but something much
more silently subversive, said into the ear of the noisy opposing
world, busy with definitions. 'The Nymph Complaining for the
Death of her Faun', unlike its title, is *not* classical, *not* erotic; its
lecherous 'faun' is merely a dying animal, its nymph is almost a
child and startlingly close to us—she speaks the poem, not as
well as the poet would; and whether all these facts make the
whole more pathetic or more ridiculous is left unconcluded,
though the poem is otherwise all conclusion. 'The Picture of
little T. C. in a Prospect of Flowers' is nearly as long, as a title,
as the poem it announces and rather grander than the little girl
to whom the poem devotes itself; but the child has large hopes
fixed on her, and perhaps also large ideas of her own dignity,
which the poem kindly undermines. That most abstractly discussed of all Marvell's poems, 'The Garden', ends by making a
reader wonder if *the* garden ever existed, outside those 'herbs
and flowers ... flowers and herbs' that help to pass the time
away.

The mid-seventeenth century was a bad time to be a private
poet in. During the wars themselves, from about 1643 till about
1647, the young Marvell—perhaps symptomatically—went on

a Grand Tour. Not long after he came home, in 1649, there occurred that event which shook the whole of Europe: the English nation cut off the head of its King. Marvell himself, the son of a fairly Calvinistical clergyman, had for a short spell as a young man inclined to the Roman church; a natural monarchist with a Royalist love of tradition, he had also a power of reason and sense of fact that moved him towards the Parliamentary position. The remaining forty years of his life would give him plenty of time to learn a poetic art that would confront the fissuring private and public worlds then coming into being: in 1650, the mid-point of the century.

Most of Marvell's public verse is now unread except by those with a professional interest in it. To appreciate it demands knowledge of the historical context which Marvell meets with such high adeptness of rhetorical skills. But there is one occasional poem which is an exception to this rule: the 'Horatian Ode upon Cromwell's Return from Ireland'. We can admire and praise this political poem, with its brilliantly adjudicated images of the condemned King and the living dictator-to-be, on the basis of a sense of history that may sometimes be founded, ironically enough, on the poem itself. It has that self-sufficiency of the true poem. Clearly, what makes it different from the other Cromwellian poems deserves to be isolated.

In the first place, the Ode poses a political conundrum. In the previous year Marvell had written three occasional poems: one addressed to Lovelace, the others lamenting the deaths of Villiers and Hastings. The sentiments of all three are to some degree or other Royalist; fiercely so in the Villiers poem, whose authorship has, however, been disputed. Some months after the 'Horatian Ode', whose date we do not know, but which is presumed to have been written in the summer of 1650, there appeared 'Tom May's Death', which certainly sounds Marvellian, and which satirized the case of a Royalist poetaster who had deserted and gone over to the Parliamentarians. A few months after this again, Marvell was living and working at Appleton House, as tutor to the daughter of Lord Fairfax, who had just resigned from the supreme command of the Parliamentary army. Given that the 'Horatian Ode' is often

referred to as a 'panegyric of Cromwell', this sandwiching com-
plication must prove suggestive. One of the things it should not
suggest, probably, is mere political opportunism on Marvell's
part. Both the poetry and the career suggest a habit of extreme
tentativeness, succeeded and explained by a habit of extreme
steadiness in commitment when once the commitment was
undertaken. When once he had undertaken public appointment
in the later 1650s Marvell stuck to the 'Good Old Cause' with a
tenacity not very usual at that point in time. In any case, the
political situation of the 1640s and '50s was so complicated as to
make such terms as 'opportunism' unsuitable. It is not simple to
change sides when there are no simple sides. This is not,
therefore, a climate in which it will prove very easy to ascertain
Marvell's attitudes in his 'Horatian Ode'; perhaps he wrote the
poem to clarify them. For it must be said that in producing work
that superficially at least belonged to the world of the public,
Marvell was committing himself to something that demanded
clear attitudes. This is why the greater part of the many critical
essays on the poem are concerned with Marvell's attitudes, ever
since the debate between Douglas Bush and Cleanth Brooks.
Bush thought the poem a relatively clear and simple panegyric
of Cromwell; Brooks found its attitudes more ambiguous, more
critical. And since their dispute, many good articles have been
written to prove that the poem's hero is Cromwell, or Charles,
or both.

In a way any critic is right who tries, as Bush did, to keep a
Marvell poem 'clear' in meaning. Brooks's reading, though far
more sensitive and understanding, perhaps ends by getting the
tone of the poem wrong: undervaluing the element in Marvell
that associates him with Jonson and with the Augustan writers
after him. Marvell seems to be always urging doubts outward,
resolving ambiguities rather than causing them. But against
Bush's conclusion, that the Ode is a simple panegyric of
Cromwell, it must be said that Cromwell would have had to be a
very naif man to be thoroughly pleased with the poem—as
pleased, for instance, as he presumably was by the 'First
Anniversary of the Government under O. C.' which Marvell
wrote five years later. And the most 'pleasing' of all these poems
is the elegy which the poet wrote on Cromwell's death. Legouis
has made the point that we learn much more about Cromwell

from the elegy than we do from the Ode, and he values the elegy for this. What we learn is certainly different in the two poems. The 'First Anniversary', like the elegy, adorns a big man with big images:

> *Cromwell* alone with greater Vigour runs,
> (Sun-like) the Stages of succeeding Suns...
>
> *Cromwell* alone doth with new Lustre spring,
> And shines the Jewel of the yearly Ring...
>
> Thou *Cromwell* falling, not a stupid Tree,
> Or Rock so savage, but it mourn'd for thee.

These two panegyrical poems were written only five and eight years after the 'Horatian Ode', but their difference in tone and style is so great as to make them seem typically 'Restoration' in mode: the effort of idealizing draws out of them a rhetoric that seems necessarily touched by the factitious, a mere dishonest avoidance of the inevitable satiric note. This is perhaps why we hear, like an echo under these lines, derisive cadences written twenty years after, derisive in effect even if Dryden's connection with Marvell's verses is only accidental:

> Shadwell alone my perfect image bears,
> Mature in dullness from his tender years;
> Shadwell alone of all my sons is he
> Who stands confirmed in full stupidity.[4]

This peculiar note—of panegyric that is a near-miss to satire—is not heard in the 'Horatian Ode'. But the reason is not that the poem is satirical already: the perfection of its courtesy is well-known. The Ode is merely incontrovertible as the 'First Anniversary' and the 'Poem upon the Death of O. C.' are not. When the 'political' Marvell calls Cromwell 'Sun-like', or describes the natural world mourning for him, or even when he gives him the tenderer praise of the elegy, the result is simply less believable than when, for instance, the same poet elsewhere shows the Mower admiring the 'sun' of his rustic face in the bright curve of his scythe, or when he makes him crossly hack down the flowers and grass precisely because they will *not* mourn for him. This difference in credibility does not, I think, derive merely from modern cynicism. Heroic idealization is always believable if believed; it is a possible, even a necessary, human experience. But Marvell is writing panegyrics of the man who has 'cut off the king's head with the crown upon it'—of the dictator who committed himself to finishing the tyranny of myth. Clarendon was to quote of the dead king, 'I have heard him often say, that if he could not live a King then he would die a Gentleman.' That Charles died a Gentleman, because he could not find a way of living as a King, was a mixture of the beautiful and the deeply discreditable— discreditable to himself first, to others after. At all events, that transition from King to Gentleman was the crux of England's political problems in the period. And it was the problem, too, of Marvell, the panegyrist of the man who was already called 'King Oliver': Marvell the political poet, whose Cromwell is a man awkwardly draped with glory as with mist.

The 'Horatian Ode', by contrast, is believable as real poems are believable. That it is so, suggests a distinction: though 'political', it is not public as the other occasional poems are public. In this sense, such debates as that of Bush and Brooks are permanently unresolvable. This is not a poem in which personalities, or attitudes to them, are primarily important; and the sense of greater freedom in the poem is the mark of Marvell's not having had to care about pleasing or displeasing this or that personality. The events of a year or eighteen months presented a crisis, it must seem, or made a kind of sense, that was beyond politics. The burden of opinionating drops from Marvell, and a different kind of thinking takes over: the Ode is beyond *attitudes*. The dropping of that burden in the 'Horatian Ode', written we must surely say as a private poem, is revealed by a small point concerning its style: a point that seems to me as important as its attitudes, though it has clearly been felt as too trivial to figure much in criticism. Most of Marvell's genuinely occasional verse is written in heroic couplets. The 'Horatian Ode' is not. It is composed in an unusual pattern of pairs of rhymed four-beat and then three-beat lines, the delicate mono-syllables of the second pair, the short lines, in effect under-cutting the first pair, changing the view, so that the stanzas seem to show the mind altering itself, moving forward again and again. This remarkable thinking metre begins with the poem's first phrases:

> The forward Youth that would appear
> Must now forsake his *Muses* dear,

Nor in the Shadows sing
His Numbers languishing.
'Tis time to leave the Books in dust,
And oyl th' unused Armours rust:
Removing from the Wall
The Corslet of the Hall.
So restless *Cromwel* could not cease. . .

The five-stressed or heroic couplet is the emerging and dominant form of the 1640s and '50s; we celebrate men like Denham or Waller simply because they helped to bring forward its bright, balanced, and public mode. Its sound and style are already enough established in Marvell's time for the ear to hear the octosyllabic or four-stressed line which he loved, as apparently lacking something. Certainly, when it was used a decade or so later by a clear and external wit like Samuel Butler, this sound of something missing is felt as apt to its indecorous or playful function. But in Marvell's hands it does not precisely have this comic note, even when it occurs—as of course it does not here—in couplet form. The thought of the 'Horatian Ode' is hardly clear and external in the Samuel Butler way; the very first lines are compressed, even distorted. The opening line means, prosaically, 'The youth who would achieve fame'; but the lilting inversion (echoed in the slightly parodic '*Muses* dear' and 'Numbers languishing') is a departure from idiom that throws important stress on that word *appear*, which implies uncertainty, reservation, perhaps illusion, and so starts the involved machine of thought going within both poem and reader. The second line—itself poetry—advocates, or at least contemplates, an abandonment of poetry, in a tone—*forsake* and *dear*—which makes this seem regrettable as well as impossible. The rhythm of the next two lines ironically climaxes the swing of the stanza by a trailing and undercutting anticlimax, blurring off into darkness with an exquisitely uncertain rhyme-word, *languishing*. These are effects unimagined by a Samuel Butler, or even by an artist as great as Ben Jonson, who wrote some beautiful octosyllabics. And the tone they achieve is not one of omission, but of reserve. Marvell is using a metre for thinking aloud in.

This metrical effect is underlined by a different aspect of the style of the Ode, one bearing on its language and syntax. Its fourth, fifth, and sixth stanzas define the violence of 'restless' Cromwell, who

> like the three-fork'd Lightning, first
> Breaking the Clouds where it was nurst,
>   Did thorough his own Side
>   His fiery way divide.
> For 'tis all one to Courage high
> The Emulous or Enemy:
>   And with such to inclose
>   Is more then to oppose.
> Then burning through the Air he went,
> And Pallaces and Temples rent:
>   And *Caesars* head at last
>   Did through his Laurels blast.

The ambiguity of Marvell's language has been a well-treated theme; and it is well illustrated by the central stanza here, drily indicating the degree to which a man of power is indifferent to friend or enemy. But the three stanzas also reveal an aspect of the diction not so much noticed, one even more interesting than mere variability in attitude. It has often been noted that Marvell leaves *cruces*, like that of the double Caesar. Charles is, and Cromwell becomes, Caesar. But whose head, precisely, here bursts through whose laurels? The crux is in fact syntactical, and depends on the fact that *blast* in this last line may be either transitive or intransitive (as 'Caesars head' is either subject or object); and we have no time, such is the poem's steady if uninsistent progress, to stop and determine which—even if the laconic metre permitted, as it does not. In this short passage alone, a number of other words share this same grammatical uncertainty, with an active or passive implication: *his own side, divide, inclose, oppose, rent.* Marvell is describing a form of natural energy perfectly recognizable, and the passage cannot be said to be truly difficult: we know very clearly what it means, and even admire the strange elegance which the smooth movement of the verse gives to an extreme destructive violence. The transitive–intransitive uncertainty merely leaves a kind of chill, a shadow across some of the most potent words. The effect is striking enough to recall a poem far in time and mood from Marvell's, in which Coleridge was to describe the condition of nightmare as one of uncertainty

> Whether I suffered, or I did;
> For all seemed guilt, remorse or woe,
> My own or others, still the same
> Life-stifling fear, soul-stifling shame.

Marvell's world is not one of nightmare. It is the achievement of his poem, as indeed of his two leading characters in it, that they raise to heroism and even to a kind of gaiety, what could otherwise have been thought of as 'shame' and 'fear'. But that doubt of 'whether I suffered, or I did' is implicit in his syntax as in his metre. In this poem, action and suffering fuse; event becomes thought; the public becomes private. This dominating impression of the poem's style is supported by a trivial point concerning the possible origin of its metre. A poem probably by the young Sir Richard Fanshawe, and existing only in manuscript, uses this anglicized Horatian metre for an interesting subject: a decision to abandon verse in order to pursue a less time-wasting and impoverished career.[5] This seems too close to 'the forward youth who would appear' to be accidental. It was perhaps the personal theme of Fanshawe's modest imitation which caught Marvell's attention, and imprinted the Horatian form in his memory as the way to make personal, public matters. For Marvell's poem can be called 'personal', almost as Fanshawe's can. Its subject is politics, as expressed through the fate of its two persons, Cromwell and Charles; the triumph of Cromwell encloses, at its centre, the opposing triumph of Charles, the triumph of death within the triumph of life. But these persons are treated with a peculiar vividness of metaphorical transformation that has the effect of removing them out of history—Charles the hunted animal netted by Cromwell, Cromwell the fierce falcon held on the lure of the falconer. Powerful contemporary figures are in fact diminished, subordinated to a third person or subject stated at the beginning and repeated, in shadowy form, at the close:

> The Forward Youth that would appear
> Must now forsake his *Muses* dear. . .
> > The same *Arts* that did *gain*
> > A *Pow'r* must it *maintain*.

If the Ode has a hero, it is finally neither Charles nor Cromwell, but an invisible man; perhaps even the 'forward youth' himself, who would (like a published poet) 'appear'. Of its two Caesars, the King and the Dictator, the poem seems to say—at the political level—something profound but simple: that the King is beautiful in defeat only, and that the Dictator who defeats him will become a King—two Caesars in one wreath. But Charles and Cromwell are also symbols of different conditions. The Ode is certainly a brilliant political poem; but the poet has extended his politics as far back as to the Rome of Lucan and Horace, and then further back still, to a time when life seems to consist only of the hunt, and the garden. And to take it that far is to take it almost out of history.

Marvell's poem has various literary sources. But there can be little doubt that its spirit is above all 'Horatian': that its style is indebted in a manner which Marvell's perfect imitation communicates as tacitly as fully. The opening two stanzas of the Ode pause at a brilliantly expressive gesture, like a gambit in chess, that of lifting armour down: an image reminiscent, though in reverse, of that which closes one of Horace's most familiar Odes, 'Quis multa gracilis' (I.v), (a poem much translated in Marvell's lifetime, by Milton and Cowley among others). The Roman poet there contemplates the thought of his sometime mistress Pyrrha's new lover, who is still held in the illusion that his delicious present moment will be his for always; and Horace then describes himself, by contrast, in the image of a man whose journey is forever ended on the sea of love, who has hung up his garments as an offering to the powerful god of the sea—

> suspendisse potenti
> vestimenta maris deo.

Whether Marvell in fact remembered this image is unimportant. His Ode is profoundly Horatian, with an artistry that has learned from many such images. Though critics have noted the Ode's Horatian context, it is usually the political attitudes which receive attention.[6] What is more striking is the effect of a whole mind and style; for it was in part the response to Horace that enabled an elsewhere intransigently 'English' and private sensibility to do what was on other terms often closed to it, to write a true poem that was also public. In another of his best-known Odes, 'Otium divos rogat' (II.xvi), Horace defines peace or detachment as not merely order in the state, but lucidity and economy of mind, the art of being 'a mind happy in the here and now', *laetus in praesens animus*. This classic theme of the Roman poet recurs often in the Odes, and outside them in the Epistles, where Horace several times uses a phrase which defines Marvell's style almost more aptly than his own: *animus aequus*, 'a mind well-balanced'.

At the end of II.xvi Horace refers to that 'small estate' where he lives, a place which becomes something like a symbol for the mind's house-in-order. If this symbol 'worked' in Horace's own poetry, and continued to haunt the imagination of Europe for many centuries, this was because the poet's verse continually made it real. What begins as a mere act of reference is paralleled by the peculiar organization and economy with which the entire poem is set in order. Horace's world is public, his tone urbane; if a sense of private personality infuses an Ode it will not be from the expression of Romantic ego, but from the pervasive, tight, and brilliant setting-in-order of objects and experiences, by which a mind is continually *laetus in praesens*, relating pasts and futures to its own steadily-advancing presentness. The impact of an Ode like 'Quis multa gracilis' comes from the dense collocation of a past and future existence which may hurt and threaten each other but which must co-exist. Indeed, the poet may be said to exist there, and with intensity, at the exact present point where the secure youth and the embittered man co-exist in one mind. Horace seems to have been perhaps the first in his language to prefer these highly original juxtapositions of words, images, and experiences, to more formal and logical sequences of thought: which is why his transitions are felt to be problematic, the subject of dispute. The art that results combines something like a maximum of the personal with a maximum of the impassive. It is not surprising to find an Ode like I.xiv, 'O navis, referent' which a reader might well take to be a classic, moving, and dry poem of ironic misery at the re-encroachment of love (and T. S. Eliot seems to have taken it as such, echoing it in his 'Marina')—firmly titled in the Loeb edition, 'To the Ship of State.'[7] Whether the Ode *is* addressed to the Ship of State, or to Horace's own battered and too-far-travelled heart is, beyond a certain point, immaterial: neither heart nor state now exist to argue about. But a poetic image has been released into history. The poem itself is a private place, a 'small estate', unshakeably individual though public in its clarity and realism. It maintains a poise that is responsible to experience, but that belongs to no one but the writer himself.

It is this quiet detachment which Marvell achieves in his 'Horatian Ode'. The poem has one direct connection with its artistic ancestor, which goes beyond its title and its metre and even the *animus aequus* always reflected in its language. Its most obvious feature is that startling poise or justice of mind that led a man writing what has been called 'a panegyric of Cromwell' to intersect the hero's victory with the king's defeat—to enclose the triumph of death within the triumph of life. The introduction of a third person, the forward youth present at the opening, permits both Cromwell and Charles to seem equidistant from us, and in a special way: the action of Charles belongs to the past, the action of Cromwell to the future. There is in Marvell's poem an organization of experience as exact and as personal as that of Horace's Odes, and this shaping is, moreover, that temporal procession of 'now, then, one day'—*nunc, antehunc, olim*—which will give an Ode by Horace its structure. Marvell's mind may here be *laetus in praesens* in a striking sense. In 1700, just half a century after the 'Horatian Ode', Dryden's *Secular Masque* would formally observe the end of an old age and the bringing-in of a new. It is possible that Marvell was in 1650 doing something very similar: that the unwonted depth and certainty of this political poem came from the unparalleled representativeness of the moment, in which a past and a future hold the human mind at a crisis reminiscent of the many human crises in time, in which losses will be as many as gains. For the execution of Charles, in the year preceding the Ode, had in fact—as we now recognize—marked the end of an era. The Middle Ages died with Charles; modernity came with the New Model Army. And the death of the King was also in some sense the end of ritual, of myth—it was the last Reformation, the final breaking of an icon: for the cult of Charles the Martyr, however long it lasted, took its intensity from its status as lost cause. The end of mythical history is an event which no poet, however rational and Protestant, can contemplate quite without disturbance. Marvell, who remained all his life

a constitutional monarchist, records something of that disturbance in the great but confused images he gives to Cromwell,
watching him

> climbe
> To ruine the great work of Time,
>   And cast the Kingdome old
>   Into another Mold.
> Though Justice against Fate complain,
> And plead the antient Rights in vain:
>   But those do hold or break
>   As Men are strong or weak.

A poet elsewhere often cool as well as witty is recording here a
degree of shock that goes well beyond what we usually mean by
the political. It reduces to triviality any superficial approach as
to what side the poet is on—where Marvell *is*; the poet is here,
at the point of shock, between past and future. The syntax of
the stanza concerning justice and fate is interestingly broken
and involute, as though the thinking of the poem checked there
in a knot before moving on again. It makes Marvell seem to be
holding for a moment a perception which could not be clearly
expressed in any of the technical languages of his time, neither
theological nor philosophical, political nor scientific. For the
peculiarity of the historical moment at which he writes is that in
it, the very concepts themselves are changing—of history, of
politics, and indeed of time itself. This is the stage of his-
toriography at which time is ceasing to begin with the garden of
Eden and end with Apocalypse; it is beginning to become the
finally unending story of the State. And, where concepts of this
scale are involved and—however obscurely—glimpsed by the
poet, it is not surprising that 'antient Rights' should be pleaded
'in vain', and the stanza drops exhausted into the mere physical
factuality of 'Men are strong or weak'. This is the Marvell who,
twenty years later in his *Rehearsal Transpros'd*, was to say of the
Civil Wars: 'Men may spare their pains when Nature is at work,
and the world will not go faster for our driving.' Conflict
resolves to the sense of process: Time, Nature, History move
on and take Charles and Cromwell with them. The poem does
not involve itself with the clash of Caesar and Caesar, as though
one could choose between them: but with the achievement and
cost of the transition in time from one to the other. It commits

itself to neither, and the deep politeness it extends to both is a
style for standing off.

Compared to even the best of the other occasional poems, the
'Horatian Ode' has the precision of a man whose probity comes
from strict reference first to himself and to his own standards; it
is in this sense a genuinely 'Protestant' poem, even a Commonwealth poem, which replaces Horace's Augustan style by
the civilized seventeenth-century conscience. Metre and diction alike become the vehicle of this precision. Each stanza,
though steady in its forward insistence, at the same time nar-
rows down to point after point of delicate awareness:

> *He* nothing common did or mean
> Upon that memorable Scene:
>   But with his keener Eye
>   The Axes edge did try:
> Nor call'd the *Gods* with vulgar spight
> To vindicate his helpless Right,
>   But bow'd his comely Head,
>   Down as upon a Bed.

This whole famous passage sparkles with sharply dangerous
words—*adorn, clap, bloody, mean, Scene, try, vulgar, helpless,
comely, Bed*—that are nails in a coffin, though whose coffin, it is
not at all easy to say. Everything is beautiful, and something is
betrayed. Rhythm underlines this uncommon aesthetic power
in the diction. The incisive, surprising rhymes that close the
oblique and devious rhythms of the 'Roman' metre—a metre so
alien to the colloquial, opinionative strength of English, and
therefore so accurate in undermining this opinionative-
ness—end by making the tone finally reserved, almost dream-
like. It may not be irrelevant that the only two really striking
poetic moments in 'The Last Instructions to a Painter' have this
same quality of dream-likeness. In one, the self-immolating
hero 'brave *Douglas*' lies down to die as one to sleep and
dream—

> Round the transparent Fire about him glows,
> As the clear Amber on the Bee does close

—and in the second, Charles II encounters in 'the dead shade of night' the ghost of England, or of Peace, and, observing her to be a female, absent-mindedly reaches out for her,

> But soon shrunk back, chill'd with her touch so cold,
> And th'airy Picture vanisht from his hold.

The 'Horatian Ode' achieves this quality of reverie far more consistently and more profoundly: but more tacitly too. There is nothing superficially Romantic in the poem. The sense of removed intensity perhaps depends initially on that oddly weighty *appear* which closes the distorted first line:

> The forward Youth that would appear.

The confused and—it may be—destructive involvement of life and literature, and of life and life, in the struggle to survive, is the subject delineated, with an extremely elegant negligence, in the poem's opening two stanzas: which drift quietly but steadily towards that critical gesture, the lifting down, for good and all, of the public armour, the defensive shell of a man. The poem begins with a submerged shock of paradox, an advised departure from the arts—art used not to conceal art but to betray it, a betrayal which is the price of that art of 'appearing'. Before Cromwell ever comes on the scene, the poem meditates on what this means, to 'appear': to live the public life. In the process substance and form are matched in a manner hardly found elsewhere in Marvell. The decorum of the Ode is peculiarly Roman, peculiarly public: hence the brilliant unity of the whole, as compared to a work like 'Appleton House', which pays its discreteness as the price of its Englishness. The Ode is a masque, almost a ballet, of pure action—of the appearance of events. We look steadily and with an unvarying equilibrium on the armour lifted down; on Cromwell not knowing friend from enemy, all alike 'inclosing' him, getting in his way; on Charles 'adorning' the scaffold, his death a mime applauded by the bloody hands of encircling soldiers—as in those theatre-deaths of criminals on the depraved late Roman stage, when life and art fused grossly into one show;[8] on the Roman 'Architects' of state running away; on the Irish 'seeing themselves tamed', like men reading their own history many years after in books or newspapers, their public commitment doing what their hearts never could—'affirming the praises', 'confessing the virtues' of the man who has destroyed them. The whole poem is a pattern of related and yet terribly different actions, a 'dream of history', with gestures caught from past and present to suggest a future, actual, probable, or possible: the armour coming down from the wall, the falcon falling heavy from the sky; Charles bowing, the Pict 'shrinking'; Caesar's head blasted, the Roman head bleeding; the bloody hands clapping, Caesar's unseen hand keeping the sword erect; and last and most, the private arts forsaken at the beginning, the public arts gaining power at the end.

These images of public life, of what we choose to call history, are all held in the scrutiny of the detached and private mind. That scrutiny reduces the conflict of the political elements to something much stiller, in which persons are 'united in the strife which divided them': so that within the poem Charles perpetually bows his head, Cromwell perpetually marches into the darkness of the future. The pattern of the whole reproduces in larger scale the continuing profundities of the simple six-syllable lines, which over and over again make the ruthless 'point' of the poem:

> those do hold or break
> As Men are strong or weak. . . .
> And yet in that the *State*
> Foresaw it's happy Fate. . . .
> How fit he is to sway
> That can so well obey. . . .

Strength and weakness, success and fear, mastery and servitude circle on each other like a roundabout; and the images playing against each other are in their turn dominated by a greater counter-image, the heartless and yet beautiful flow of the poem's 'action', its circling, rhyming but steadily advancing passage through time. The poem unanswerably subordinates the arts of its beginning to the arts of its close. In this sense there is no doubt at all that the poem is 'about' Cromwell: for Cromwell is in it the fact that constitutes the future, and Marvell's is a mid-century, even a Restoration intelligence, for whom facts matter. But there is a fine artistry in the way the poem moves with full momentum towards that disturbing close: where Cromwell, himself now grown into Caesar, the now personally nameless as well as faceless 'son of War and Fortune', must march indefatigably on and on and on, like Time itself, into a future that is after all factless, unknown, and void:

> And for the last effect
> Still keep thy Sword erect:
> Besides the force it has to fright
> The Spirits of the shady Night,
> The same *Arts* that did *gain*
> A *Pow'r* must it *maintain*.

The pauses between 'fright' and 'The Spirits', between '*gain*' and 'A *Pow'r*', are like hesitations, difficult decisions; and the continuity between them, as the poem moves none the less on, is like a walk out into darkness on a raised high wire. These are 'effects', to use Marvell's own impassive word, which take the poem a long way beyond what we usually expect of political panegyric.

This best of Marvell's political poems takes its depth from its capacity to cut through the historic and to go down to a level which we do not usually intend when we name the 'political'. To some degree this can be thought of as the particular gift of Marvell, the obverse of what appears in other forms as an unsociable reserve and reticence, even eccentricity of mind; to some degree also it is the faculty of all real poetic intelligence to undercut the mundane in this way. But it is also an aspect of the historical moment when Marvell was writing. Writers of the mid-century were both privileged and burdened by living through a phase of history so critical as almost to seem archetypal. Political history in the penumbra of the Civil Wars, from about 1640 on to about 1690, can appear to be 'complete', as though statecraft were an experience as finite as chess, and as though everything that could possibly happen in political organization actually occurred then, once and for all. The most intelligent and conscious men of the time seem almost to have recognized this archetypal quality in their experience, partly voiced by Cowley's famous and bitter lament that a 'warlike, various and tragical age' was 'best to *write of*, but worst to *write in*': for the history of the time always, at its deepest, moves towards the dream-like, tragic, or mythical. The greatest case is of course *Paradise Lost*, which is—among other things—the history of Milton's own lifetime; but the same might be said of the more exalted of his own prose works, or of the quality of tragic fiction or heroic romance which lights up Clarendon's great *History*, and which still survives as a faint resonance of the sublime even in Dryden's mock-heroic treatments of his own age. At this point in time, the political was still fully open to the interpretations of it made by the whole man. Academic studies often assume that 'history' must mean constitutional history, and will be best assessed by the politically-minded in the modern sense. But this is itself historically questionable. History as a game of power, on a secular field free from religious sanctions, is a definition familiar only to a post-Machiavellian world; but Hobbes's *Leviathan* was not yet published when Marvell's Ode was written, and politics becomes the modern rivalry of factions only with the Restoration. Marvell's Ode seems even consciously transitional in this, as in so many other ways: for this transformation of public life into an arena that could be called political in a more narrow sense, seems to be a submerged apprehension of Marvell's poem, one of the profoundly disturbing transitions that will come with the returning Cromwell. For Cromwell is the greatest of those 'forward youths' that would 'appear', killing the king and replacing ritual with power.

It is the strength of the Ode that the intensity of the moment's crisis, as Marvell apprehended it, empowered him to cut down to a level that most of the other political poems do not reach to. That the age did not in general invite it, that the Muses *were* betrayed, is a fact which the Ode both states and counter-acts. Marvell can write extremely distinguished political poetry only at a level of private awareness that the public did not in general desire. But the reverse of this is, oddly enough, operative. If we are content to allow our sense of what may constitute the political to extend as widely as the time in fact permitted for minds so inclined, then Marvell's most private poems will over and over again throw light on the actual history of the age. And it is here, I think, that the explanation lies of that peculiar sense of scale in some of the poet's best lyrics. They cut deep into their age. The ways in which they do so may be at once and intuitively apprehended in the reading: for the reading mind may make instant references and comparisons over an extremely wide area, hardly aware that it does so, but acting by a huge system of latent codes and brief hieroglyphics. To make this process articulate and rational is not easy, and would take a quantity of time and space that would prove neither possible nor—if possible—very interesting. It might be better, therefore, to proceed simply by sketching in one or two mere suggestions as to why and how it is that we find this quality of historical depth in Marvell's lyrics.

Marvell's poetry is usually assumed to have been mostly written in the 1650s. There is reason to question this as a matter of fact, but it remains true that the 1640s and '50s are crucial to the poet's experience: his mind was formed by them. This period, and that longer age which contains it, are most often thought of as an age of conflict—a century of revolution. Obviously there is sense in this. But the people who lived through the period often seem to have felt very differently. The most famous story to have survived the wars—probably apocryphal, and the more suggestive for it—is that of the peasant who, ordered off the field of battle at Edgehill, expressed some surprise and interest that the parties in question were engaged in arms. This lowly reaction is peculiarly reflected in one of the most insistent themes or myths of the more exalted Clarendon's *History of the Rebellion*, his stubborn recreation of the great golden peace of the Caroline period, so suddenly and so nightmarishly violated. Below the experience of rational conflict in the Civil War period is something much deeper and more humanly real: bewilderment, a sense of the violation of the natural, an attachment to a far longer historical past, in the perspective of which 'such things do not happen'. The experience of 'Though Justice against Fate complain' is perhaps not a sense of conflict, but its opposite—a bewilderment at the absence of clear issues, a tragi-comic sense of the withdrawal of the rational. The War itself had been 'this war without an enemy'. This is the phrase, now a famous one, which the Parliamentarian Sir William Waller used in a letter explaining to a great friend who was a Royalist that he could no longer meet him. Waller's sense of the irrationality—yet hardly meaninglessness—of the pressures that were driving them both emerges in his description of the

Wars as both 'this tragedy', and yet *Opus Domini*, the work of the Lord.

Waller's image of the Wars is representative of the feeling of all the moderates of his time—which means the greater number of sane and conscientious English gentlemen. They felt themselves held in an impasse, a tragedy that was none the less fated, necessary, godly: and they felt it similarly whether they were nominally of the Parliamentarians or the Royalists. But the time was governed by men who were not moderate. Marvell in his Ode confronts, as though face to face with each other, the two men who almost certainly never met, Charles and Cromwell. It could be said that the vocation of Charles, like the instincts of most of the Stuarts, was so absolutely to define the nature of Kingship as to make most of his subjects have to choose between betraying themselves and betraying their country. And the vocation of Cromwell was absolutely to stop him doing it: to 'cut off the king's head with the crown upon it'. Since the age could scarcely manage without a king, the process was also to some degree self-betraying, even in the case of King Charles and King Oliver. In April 1646, Charles escaped from Oxford disguised as a servant: the Royalist poet Cleveland commemorated the event with his *Kings Disguise*, whose dozens of conceits make over and over again the one simple embittered point:

> Oh for a State-distinction to arraigne
> *Charles* of high Treason 'gainst my Soveraigne.

This process of self-betrayal, enforced by the historical milieu, is generic to all the greater literature of the age. It affects Milton's Adam as deeply as it does that little group of aristocrats who gather at Great Tew in the Royalist Clarendon's *History of the Rebellion*; cultivated, rational, and peace-loving individuals fighting off the knowledge of evil in the world outside, and becoming, in the writer's hands, almost an image of the betrayal by History of the innocent intellect itself. Many of Clarendon's heroes rode into battle despairing; some died unarmed. The pattern of Royalist death in the Civil Wars is epitomized in Clarendon's account of the fall of the King's standard-bearer, Sir Edmund Verney, who rode into battle at Edgehill unarmed and undefended, because he was fighting for a king whose cause he did not respect:

I do not like the quarrel, and do heartily wish that the King would yield and consent to what they desire; so that my conscience is only concerned in Honour and Gratitude to follow my Master.

In terms of 'cause' and 'conflict', Verney died defending bishops whose rights he did not believe in. But not only Royalists died bewildered. The best of the surviving Parliamentarians had only to wait a few years to feel equally betrayed by the execution of their King, whose powers—diminished and reformed—many had believed themselves to be fighting for. (It was Lady Fairfax, the wife of the great Parliamentarian leader who was also Marvell's 'patron', who shouted out in rage from the public gallery as the King was sentenced at his trial.) And after ten years more, they could feel equally betrayed by the King's Restoration; for the reign of Charles II not only undid what the religious principles of the Commonwealth achieved, but even abandoned the patriarchal habits of the Caroline period before it.

The mid-seventeenth century called into being, in response to historical changes going back many generations, all-or-nothing intensities which the actual politics of the time could do little but betray. Marvell himself, in his *Rehearsal Transpros'd*, speaks of 'that imaginary absolute government, upon which rock we all ruined'. To put it another way, it was the age of Paradise Lost: an age in which Paradise was never more clearly perceived than at the exact moment at which it ceased to be believed in. In political terms, *Eikon Basilike*—the holy image of the King—appeared almost as soon as the King was executed (as Marvell's Cromwell is called 'Caesar'); and the image of Charles in the famous frontispiece of that work of hagiography brings together at once all the time's impossibilities, reverently haloing an exquisite monarch whose eyes are directed upwards to an air-borne crown. It has been noticed that Charles looked sad long before he had good reason to; that the portraits fashioned by Van Dyck throughout the 1630s gave the King a lustrous melancholy owing perhaps less to spirituality than to the high style of aristocratic and indeed imperial portraiture from which they derived.[9] And even the idealizing court masques of the time are gestures of royal power. It is hard now not to find the 'mask' of the King in the *Eikon Basilike* simply too high-bred, too sophisticated, too late in time for a holy image: Charles can merely *act* it, with a grace that is only just not condescension, and that Marvell in his Ode catches with a perfect dryness:

> *He* nothing common did or mean
> Upon that memorable Scene.

Much later in time, at the end of the 1660s, Marvell comes to write about Charles's eldest son, in his satire on 'our Lady State', 'The Last Instructions to a Painter': and his Eikon of the son is as clear-eyed as that of the father. Having failed to seduce the ghost of England, Charles II bustles off to meet his chosen associates:

> To her own Husband, *Castlemain*, untrue.
> False to his Master *Bristol, Arlington*;
> And *Coventry*, falser than any one,
> Who to the Brother, Brother would betray;
> Nor therefore trusts himself to such as they.

That betrayal which Shakespeare's stage kings, his Richard or his Lear, had experienced as a sin of the private heart, becomes at last in Marvell's Restoration satires a rule of the political game.

Marvell's best poems lie within a territory that charts out the transition from one field to the other. The Elizabethan sense of tragic involvement has ebbed; the Restoration sense of comic ruthlessness has hardly yet developed. Marvell writes within a period of time in which political events are still only a shadow of other experiences. The bewilderment of the age seems unconsciously to have reflected the modern recognition that the English Wars were, in fact, only the surface symptom of a temporal transition beginning generations earlier, and not to be categorized into any single one *casus belli*, ecclesiastical, economic, or sociological. The Wars were merely the temporal focus of the meeting of new and old. Sir William Waller, caught up in the 'war without an enemy', living through a tragedy which is none the less *Opus Domini*, sees, as it were, through and behind the War itself, a deeper war intrinsic to the mere passage of time. The appalling sense of unreality which came to many men like him may explain curious incidents like the ghost-battles in the night-sky after Edgehill, when all the sounds of

battle were re-enacted for shepherds and passers-by.[10] The War
itself was a kind of ghost, hardly believed in even by the
combatants who died in it: a momentary nightmare, in which
past and future were caught together as in Hobbes's evocation
of the ghostly present moment:

the prognostics of time to come . . . are naturally but conjectures upon
experience of time past.

In this context it is striking that Marvell should have opened
the major political poem which succeeds the 'Horatian Ode', the
'First Anniversary', with an image that extends the milieu of his
benevolent dictator, Cromwell, across a natural field both
enormous and generically destructive:

> Like the vain Curlings of the Watry maze,
> Which in smooth streams a sinking Weight does raise;
> So Man, declining alwayes, disappears
> In the weak Circles of increasing Years;
> And his short Tumults of themselves Compose,
> While flowing Time above his Head does close.

The fault of the 'First Anniversary' is that Cromwell's actual
activities never give Marvell a chance, imaginatively, to impose
the dictator's image upon that tremendous field glimpsed at
first: Cromwell the Ruler refuses to 'go down' humanly, without convincing us that he 'stays up' superhumanly, and the
poem, therefore, never sounds true. But its opening affords
an instance of what would, for Marvell, constitute a
truth—political or otherwise—to which he could respond with
imaginative certainty. His image of the destructive 'Watry
maze' brings to mind the fact that 'politics' are only one aspect of
that larger disturbance which troubled the whole century, and
changed the dimensions of the past behind it and the future
before it. The fatalism of these lines reminds us that many of
Marvell's contemporaries believed deeply that the world was
drawing to an end, running down in self-disintegrating exhaus-
tion. And since the old Renaissance Europe was crumbling
around them, they were in a way right. It is difficult to read
much in later Renaissance literature without coming to share
this sense of a culture that is gradually, like our own, dying on
its feet. But a new more scientific culture was emerging as the

old faded. If we translate this double sense of threshold and collapse into an outward-looking, classical image of Nature as a whole, then we arrive at the image of the stream of 'flowing' Time, in the 'First Anniversary': a Time that is always beginning as it ends, as the metre of the 'Horatian Ode' flows on from conclusive rhyme to rhyme, and ends with the word *maintain*.

Marvell's lifetime was a meeting of old and new in a sense more specific than this. It was the destructive wars themselves that helped to create new studies. A historian of the Society of Antiquaries tells us that

soldiers on the King's side of the warring armies used their enforced travels to take antiquarian notes. Richard Symonds's *Diary of the Marches of the Royal Army During the Great Civil War* includes many notes on churches, chiefly heraldic.[11]

It is easy to imagine Charles's lace-collared knights carefully annotating the ruins as Cromwell's leather-jacketed forward-looking colonels everywhere added to them. Other new studies and techniques originated in the civil wars: the Royal Society began from wartime meetings of refugee scholars; the lively accounts of military events in wartime Cavalier journalism helped to generate both the characteristic style of Restoration comedy and the prose fiction of men like Defoe.[12] But it is antiquarianism in general which most reflects that involvement of old and new characterizing the period, a delighted power of insight brought about directly by the crumbling of a betrayed past. The best prose writer in this new antiquarianism, death and new life oddly blending in his work, is of course Sir Thomas Browne: 'Time hath endless rarities' in the remarkable last chapter of his *Urn Burial*. But Browne's mosaic vision is endemic, in much simpler form, to the whole mid- and later-seventeenth century. The antiquarian, historian, and biographer John Aubrey can be found writing a note on the ruins of Malmesbury Abbey, which absorbs politics into history and history into one great green landscape:

Where the Choir was, now grass grows, where anciently were buried Kings and great men.[13]

And towards the end of the century the traveller Celia Fiennes was moved to an unaccustomed poetry by what she saw:

Grass grows now where Winchelsea was, as was once said of Troy.[14]

Andrew Marvell is a special kind of antiquarian poet. He has
a peculiar attentiveness to the whole literary life of the age,
borrowing here and there with an absorbed eclecticism, and
seeming to throw off a perfected specimen of every form that
offered. It is noticeable, however, that Marvell is a 'finisher',
that his beautiful lyrics produce the effect of making every form
seem incapable of further development: each is the last in its
line. What Marvell does to it, sets it in amber. But other poets
than Marvell were antiquarian. Herrick and Lovelace are
equally men enchanted by the small, preservers of the minutiae
of cultural history, with their anciently-traditioned Anacreontic
poems on the Grasshopper, the Fly, the Ant, the Snail—

> Compendious Snayl! Thou seem'st to me
> Large Euclid's strict epitome.

If Marvell, with all his concentration on the small, is neverthe-
less obscurely larger than even such excellent fellow-
miniaturists as Herrick and Lovelace, this is because his
imagination sustains such antiquarianism more consistently
and more profoundly. His poems, which may be seen as a
virtuoso's elegy for a whole past tradition that is crumbling into
fragments, are at the same time faithful to a new vision of that
Nature which, like Time, flows overhead as Man goes down.
'Grass grows now where Winchelsea was': so Marvell takes his
visitor down into the meadows beyond the historic Appleton
house, where the grasshoppers laugh down on men:

> They, in there squeking Laugh, contemn
> Us as we walk more low then them:
> And, from the Precipices tall
> Of the green spir's, to us do call.

Such lines as these give Marvell at his best: a man private,
idiosyncratic, strange. But these private qualities at the same
time seem to render the real life of the age quite as truly as do the
lucid externalities of the 'Horatian Ode'. The meadows in question after all belonged to Lord Fairfax, sometime head of the
Parliamentary army, a man of equal public and private honour:
who had retired to his estate—into *his* 'privateness' and
'strangeness'—because he could not face that invasion of

Scotland which Marvell in his Ode so impassively recommends
to Fairfax's some-time second-in-command. Fairfax found that
he had reached, as it were, his personal maximum of betrayal,
and elected as a result to step for the time being out of 'history'.
Marvell's green world appears to be at the opposite pole, in its
playful quasi-pastoralism, from the urgent world of affairs; but
it intersects just as well the inward consciousness of the time,
the divergent creative mind that drove men then—as much as
now—to do what they did.

In his 'First Anniversary', a public enough poem, Marvell
described history as the waters closing over a man's head. The
meadows of Lord Fairfax's house are the place where we go
down:

> To see Men through this Meadow Dive,
> We wonder how they rise alive.
> As, under Water, none does know
> Whether he fall through it or go.
> But, as the Marriners that sound,
> And show upon their Lead the Ground,
> They bring up Flow'rs so to be seen,
> And prove they've at the Bottom been.

It is hard not to read into these lines an almost Symbolist image
of poetry as the reward of the death in life. Perhaps Marvell
meant that; or perhaps his imagination was affected by something closer to his own time, a new archaeologizing, antiquarian
spirit that was developing startlingly far and fast. Aubrey has a
note that seems a brilliant prevision of Victorian geology, vis-
ualizing the world under an Ocean that ebbed to leave the earth
exposed and fishy:[15] there is something of this in Marvell's
flooded meadow; and his image of meadow-flowers at the bottom of the sea makes one wonder if he had seen North Sea
fishermen bringing up land-flowers from the sea-bed. The
Humber, near which he had spent much of his youth, and
which had drowned his father, is an extremely ancient river,
that flowed before the North Sea covered the land. However
small the chosen areas of Marvell's poems, they often turn out to
be surprisingly extensive in this way. Where they don't go
wide, they go deep: like Lord Fairfax's mowers, who step into a
meadow, and drown in the sea of time, or of history, or merely
of the mind. The poet's green world is charged with that new

intuition which made Aubrey insist that 'the World is much older than is commonly supposed', that 'these Antiquities are so exceeding old that no Bookes do reach them'.[16] But where Aubrey was a scholar and even a scientist, Marvell was an artist; and it is not the visible world alone, that 'Pomegranat full of cavernes' as Aubrey called it, which holds the poet's attention. It is the depths of the mind, a world within and yet beyond the dying culture of his time, which become Marvell's subject: a green world always extending like an abyss within the formal enclosures of the age, its intuitions of a 'wild and fragrant innocence' coming to rebuke the high-walled garden.

In February 1656, late in the Interregnum, a minor but interesting event occurred in London. A company of soldiers under orders from Colonel Pride, the High Sheriff of Surrey, came to the Hope Theatre (once used for both plays and bear-baiting but long abandoned by the actors), led out all the bears, and shot them dead. A diarist of the time records that the troopers left alive only 'one white innocent cub'.[17] Such incidents must have been frequent in the war period itself: Aubrey tells a tragi-comic anecdote of soldiers shooting an old man's pet gander, which was exactly the same age as the man himself. But the wartime stories, usually involving Royalist troops, suggest no more than the ordinary brutality of their military context. The incident of the bears has some further resonance that makes it stay in the mind, seeming to communicate an oddly acute sense of life as it actually was in the empty squares and market-places of Commonwealth London. This is because the event holds in itself, as so much pre-Restoration history does, the lineaments of the psychological meaning the whole period has taken on for us. It embodies, in a small symbol at once savage and grotesque, all the time's impossibility. Which is better or worse: to bait bears or to shoot them? The decisive gesture proved futile: both bear-baiting and play-acting came back with the Restoration. But not to the empty Hope Theatre, which was turned into tenements. Time had after all moved on.

Just as this crude event of the bears can in itself appear to symbolize so much that was actual in the political choices or impossibilities of the period, so Marvell's tender and ironically beautiful poems can be reminiscent of a whole historical past.

His 'Nymph complaining for the death of her Faun' is itself a
historical event (it figured in a lifetime) that goes one stage
further in its power to reflect the world around it. It is an
invention, not a happening; it says more, and more truthfully.
Marvell makes his poem catch its heroine in a moment of real
time, which he deliberately relates to the public life of the age:

> The wanton Troopers riding by
> Have shot my Faun and it will dye.

Everything that happens in this poem takes place between the
past of 'Have shot' and the future of 'will dye'. And this acute
temporality is echoed in a fact that accounts of the poem sometimes scarcely bother to notice. The 'Nymph Complaining' is a
masterpiece of travesty on the part of a tough, highly literate
Yorkshireman, the present or future M.P. for Hull and satirist
of Charles II's government. The poet completely disappears
into the precise voice of a girl, its bad grammar, its baby syntax:
all the bravely quavering chant of a well-brought-up young
innocent, now robbed of her innocence, but doing what she can
with what is left. To recognize the travesty is to measure the
distance—which is also a closeness—between the poet and the
child, which is also, in its turn, a way of knowing from the
beginning that something is finished. The nymph is done for as
much as her fawn. The girl is childish, the fawn after all a
spoiled pet, chewing up the roses and trampling the garden; no
wonder Sylvio got tired and went. All the same the lines are an
exquisite elegy as well as a comedy, and the white statue of the
fawn is almost an icon: a fragile icon, but not yet quite broken.

   A poem like 'The Nymph complaining for the death of her
Faun' seems to hold together for a moment, late in time, some of
the fragmenting private and public feelings that mattered most
in the seventeenth century: and it does it the more intensely for
its own triviality. A small thing may symbolize more adequately
than a large, given the right reticence and absence of egoism in
the artist; it commits itself to the imagination of a reader.
Marvell may be said, in the end, to represent or commemorate
his age, not by such traces of 'conflict' as may be found in his
work, but by these reconciling, elusive (perhaps treacherous)
symbols. The importance of conflict in his work can be greatly
overstated; Marvell is the least dramatic of poets, and always

has difficulty in either animating or concluding his dialogue poems. It is not debate or revolution which really interest or disturb him, but the necessity of compromise and reconciliation, the habit of loyalty and the nature of tradition. He seeks to find images that will express coherently the fusions and confusions of existence in history, with the self always hopeful, always betraying and betrayed:

> fetter'd ...
> In Feet; and manacled in Hands.
> Here blinded with an Eye; and there
> Deaf with the drumming of an Ear ...
>
> So Architects do square and hew,
> Green Trees that in the Forest grew.

Marvell may be said, therefore, to be most himself, *and* most capable of mediating a truth of his time, through images and poems whose relation to their time is only that oblique relation of the house or the church to the green tree in the forest. As a poet, he throws light—if this is the kind of light we want from a poet—on the constitutional history of his time, and the massive changes in the development of bureaucracy, by effects as reticent as (for instance) his transformation of pastoral. 'The second temple was not like the first': Marvell brought new life to pastoral by the mocking energy with which he killed it off. What appear to be his early love-pastorals, though few are datable, give the impression of having been written, with great brilliance of style, one day after their conventions of language and feeling finally ceased to be tolerable. The shepherd and shepherdess Thyrsis and Dorinda, being converted to Christianity, blissfully depart to commit suicide by opium; Daphnis abandons his agonized suit to Chloe at the moment when she begins to relent, and takes up a career of promiscuity. Like his Petrarchan love poems, 'The Gallery' and 'The Unfortunate Lover', these pastorals can make the conventions they use seem dated beyond belief, and yet these same conventions still exert power over the mind: as though Marvell's characters were trapped, with one foot in the past, one in the future. The grotesquerie of all these works—which are brilliant, but uncomfortable—is resolved in the creation of the Mower, Marvell's highly original invention. The Mower is less a character than an elusive new convention who voices some of Marvell's most individual apprehensions. As strong as a peasant, as polite as a courtier and as vulnerable as a child, the Mower may well be Marvell-the-poet as seen by Marvell-the-politician. All the old pastoral props have been diminished and then naturalized into that world of small creatures that fill the Mower poems: the hot grasshoppers, the green frog wading in the brook, the night-ingale reading music all the summer night long, the 'darling Daffadils' and thrusting grass itself. It is a brilliant toy world that reflects, as in a glass, the reflecting consciousness, perhaps equally small, of the Mower in love, labouring, philosophizing, grieving, scolding, chopping himself down with his own scythe, and always singing as he does it. If Milton's 'Lycidas' shows how powerfully an artist may use the pastoral conventions of the late Renaissance, then Marvell's 'Mower to the Glo-worms' shows how quietly such conventions may be undercut.

To recall Marvell's great contemporary, a colleague and friend who also learned how to transform politics into poetry, is to sharpen the sense of what is individual to the author of the Mower poems. Milton too can be the most ravishing of verbal artists; but his genius needed space. Full as it is of detailed brilliance, *Paradise Lost* needs all its twelve books to make its point: it is not finished until all its massive length has arrived at that final 'solitary way'. Marvell was at home in small poems. 'The Mower to the Glo-worms' imparts a sense of a lost para-dise—irretrievably, if in the end lightly lost—not qualitatively less deep than any comparable moment in Milton. Marvell can even do this with a single word. It would be fanciful to say that the poet compacts most of what was important in the history of his time into the way he uses the word *green*, but such a claim would not be meaningless. The longest of his unsatirical poems, 'Appleton House', tends to rely for its form and mass on con-ventions and circumstances now not too easy to retrieve from their past moment, but we continue to make the attempt because of the life that floods the poem once the poet moves to the meadows, where the water has ebbed from the cut grass:

> For now the Waves are fal'n and dry'd,
> And now the Meadows fresher dy'd;
> Whose Grass, with moister colour dasht
> Seems as green Silks but newly washed.

To call 'green silks'—like 'green thought'—a Metaphysical image, is only to gesture at the degree of power some poets managed to get into certain conjunctions of words at a given moment of history: conjunctions that, without exception, reflect shock, disjunction, reconciliation.[18] Marvell's 'green' is always the colour of a concept, almost an act of faith in some possibility of the natural that transcends and outgoes the most destructive sense-experience, as the grass, mown, for a moment is green silk. To conceptualize in this way Marvell will empty out his lines around the word *green*, or associate green with grass, or with glitter, or with brook- or sea-water, or will abstract his *green* or *grass* by comparing it to hope, or to miracle, or by calling grass *green* only as days may be called *golden*. In the mowing of the meadows, which fugitively and at deliberate distance reflects the history of its period—so that a dead king diminishes, impossibly, to a small slashed bird—the mind, or the soul, or Time, or Nature, or merely grass, gets itself resurrected as *green silks*: an image that exquisitely radiates all the fastidious connoisseurship of the period, like a rarity that catches the light a long way away and a long time ago.

The single poem which has most of this quality is the haunting but elusive 'Bermudas'. Part icon, part ironic or even comic elegy, this is in some ways Marvell's most perfect poem, though less popular now than among the Victorians, who probably responded to its charm without letting its deep irony disturb their reading. In the early 1650s Marvell lodged with one John Oxenbridge, who had in 1634 been turned out of his Oxford college for Puritan practices and had gone to the Bermudas, ending his long if interrupted spell there by becoming governor of the Islands. Marvell's poem is likely to have some connection with Oxenbridge's experience of the Islands, which was troubled by disruption and not idyllic; the same detached connection, perhaps, as the poem seems to have with a longish poem by Waller on the Islands, a piece of more or less mock-heroic description in heroic couplets. Marvell's relationship with any apparent sources is likely to be of an extreme detachment, just as the poem may have been written, I think, many years after the early 1650s. Like 'The Nymph Complaining' and 'The Garden', 'Bermudas' has a philosophical quality that suggests middle-age, not youth. It is the most detached,

dissociated of poems, though its central experience is tenderly
involved. The chief part of the poem is a hymn of praise and
thanks that comes from a small boat: and this boat is discovered
caught in a mysterious and tropical calm, which in effect divides
the singing from us as if by glass. The opening quatrain builds a
frame or barrier containing, and cutting off from us, the poem's
lyric substance:

> Where the remote Bermudas ride
> In th' Oceans bosome unespy'd,
> From a small Boat, that row'd along,
> The listning Winds receiv'd this Song.

If the Bermudas are *remote* we are not near them; if they or the
ocean's bosom are *unespied* we do not see them; if the *listning
Winds receive* the song we do not hear it; if there are individual
persons in the boat we are not told of them. The boat moves, it
is unclear where, and the song rises, it is unclear from whom or
to whom—indeed, it seems unclear to the singers themselves,
whoever they are, for they throw their thanks up at

> Heavens Vault,
> Which thence (perhaps) rebounding, may
> Eccho beyond the *Mexique Bay*.

As the song ends, the boat moves away, in no stated direction
but—so it seems—that of the clock:

> Thus sung they, in the *English* boat,
> An holy and a chearful note,
> And all the way, to guide their Chime,
> With falling Oars they kept the time.

The first line of this last quatrain, 'Thus sung they, in the
English boat', always brings a faint and reassuring shock in the
reading, late in the poem: it seems to be one of Marvell's
beloved anti-climactic climaxes. There *is* someone in the boat
after all: and the boat is, of all things—considering the exotic
circumstances—an *English* boat; and the vision they have sung
about is not only *holy*, it is *chearful*. The effect is rather as
though Ariel had turned out to be a practising Methodist. With
a transition as profound as a change of key in music, the last
quatrain roots a dream in reality. For the singers are without

doubt involved in a vision of Paradise. They may be going to or from the Bermudas, but it is Paradise that they see:

> He hangs in shades the Orange bright,
> Like golden Lamps in a green Night,
> And does in the Pomgranates close,
> Jewels more rich than *Ormus* show's.
> He makes the Figs our mouths to meet;
> And throws the Melons at our feet,
> But Apples plants of such a price,
> No Tree could ever bear them twice.

Waller's descriptive couplets had praised without convincing. Marvell's abbreviated medium transforms the other poet's images by dramatizing them into the monosyllables of innocence. The gratitude sounds childish—Paradise is a heavenly garden-fête, hung with paper lanterns, shining late at night. But the sophistication and control of the recording mind, Marvell's unerring instinct for the central unsatisfied delight, converts that childishness into an intense wistfulness permanently human, a longing from which the habitual scepticism is almost withheld, except, it may be, in the dryness of 'such a price'. So long as they sing and row, those in the small boat are in the presence of, if not Paradise, then at least an image of it. But that 'so long as' is bounded, as the song itself is framed, by the mysterious void all around. The poem catches the small boat and holds it for a moment out at sea, locked in this silence of the unheard, the unseen: a silence that allows to lapse into a real doubt the rhetorical question with which the singers begin:

> What should we do but sing his Praise
> That led us through the watry Maze,
> Unto an Isle so long unknown,
> And yet far kinder than our own?

In his 'First Anniversary' it is Time that Marvell calls a 'watry Maze'. A moment of time, of history, holds his singers where they are. With such a context, the outcome could always have been different—could always *be* different, in so far as the poem is present and alive. Paradise exists, then, only in the singers' marvellous, doubtful image of it.

In the 'Bermudas', Marvell takes a green world somewhere far out of sight, and finds it at the centre; he writes a hymn so private as to be essentially inaudible, and it echoes 'beyond the *Mexique Bay*'. This public art of the private dream is a reversal of that impulse by which in the 'Horatian Ode' Marvell makes a private legend out of public events and persons. His Bermudan singers praise God for turning oranges into 'golden Lamps in a green Night'. The phrase will do very well for the creative transformations of Marvell's own poetry.

NOTES

1. See, for instance, Elsie Duncan-Jones's brilliant 'A Great Master of Words: Some Aspects of Marvell's Poems of Praise and Blame', (*Proceedings of the British Academy*, 1975).
2. Joseph H. Summers gives some good reasons for scepticism about the generally accepted chronology of Marvell's poems in *The Heirs of Donne and Jonson* (O.U.P. New York, 1970), pp. 160–2. In the lecture already cited, Mrs. Duncan-Jones suggests that the 'high palaces of kings' in 'Hortus' would, if taken literally, point to a time after Marvell frequented the palace of Westminster.
3. On the subject of 'public' poetry in general, and Marvell's in particular, see, e.g., in addition to Summers, Patrick Cruttwell's *The Shakespearian Moment* (Columbia U.P., 1954) and L. C. Knights's *Public Voices* (Chatto, 1971).
4. A. L. Korn argues that Dryden is here echoing the description of Abdon in *Davideis IV*: '*Mac Flecknoe* and Cowley's *Davideis*', *Essential Articles for the study of John Dryden*, ed. H. T. Swedenberg, Jr. (1966), pp. 170–200. It seems to me possible that there is some relationship between Cowley's lines and Marvell's in the 'First Anniversary', and that Dryden, whose lines are verbally closer to Marvell's, is here remembering both poets.
5. William Simeone, 'A Probable Antecedent of Marvell's Horatian Ode', *Notes and Queries*, 197 (1952), pp. 316–18.
6. The best study is John S. Coolidge's 'Marvell and Horace', *Modern Philology*, 63 (1965), pp. 111–20.
7. E. Fraenkel argues that the Ode must be allegorical and that its Hellenic background, together with early interpretations of it, suggest that it refers to *res publica*; he adds, however: 'Horace preferred not to lift at any point the veil of the allegory' (*Horace*, Oxford 1957, pp. 154–6).
8. As in Massinger's *Roman Actor* (1626).
9. Roy Strong, *Van Dyck's 'Charles I on Horseback'* (Lane, 1972).
10. See, e.g., Peter Young, *Edgehill 1642* (Roundwood Press, 1967), pp. 162–6.
11. Joan Evans, *A History of the Society of Antiquaries* (Oxford, 1956), p. 21.
12. Cf. C. V. Wedgwood, *Seventeenth-Century English Literature* (Oxford, 1950), pp. 96–8; also P. W. Thomas, *Sir John Berkenhead* (Oxford,

1969), pp. 127–8: 'Royalists' literary activities, far from being crushed in the Interregnum, were stimulated by the changed conditions. The *esprit de corps* built up in the years of warfare was not dissipated but in some respects consolidated. . . . Indeed, what they saw as the triumph of anarchy and iconoclasm made them more than ever conscious of their destiny as guardians of all things precious and noble in the world of letters.'

13. John Aubrey, *Wiltshire: The Topographical Collections*, ed. J. E. Jackson, (1862), p. 255.

14. *The Journeys of Celia Fiennes*, ed. Christopher Morris (1949), p. 138.

15. John Aubrey, *Three Prose Works*, ed. John Buchanan-Brown (Centaur Press, 1972), p. 317.

16. Aubrey, *Wiltshire*, p. 318.

17. See J. Q. Adams, *Shakespearean Playhouses* (1920), p. 337; Leslie Hotson, *Commonwealth and Restoration Stage* (1928), pp. 59–70 ('Bear Gardens and Bear-Baiting').

18. Marvell's phrase perhaps recalls Milton's line in *Comus*: 'That in their green shops weave the smooth-haired silk' (l.715).

IV

MARVELL OUR CONTEMPORARY

by Muriel Bradbrook

THERE is a special sense in which at this tercentenary celebration we may speak of Marvell our Contemporary. Recognition of the supremacy of his art, by which two or three of his lyrics set a gold standard for all other lyrics in the language to be tested by—this recognition is just fifty-seven years old. Marvell, as we know him today, arrived in 1921, in the course of the celebrations for the tercentenary of his birth. In the changing fashions of these years, the supremacy then rather surprisingly and decisively conferred on him has never been challenged. Marvell is perhaps the one poet who *never* gets devalued, is never made the victim of a critical axe-job.

True, before this Tennyson had persuaded Palgrave to put a couple of poems into *The Golden Treasury* which 'Q' in *The Oxford Book of English Verse* increased to half a dozen; but this hardly prepared anyone for the declaration in 1921 by the great editor of Donne, Sir Herbert Grierson, that Marvell at his best excelled Donne and Dryden;[1] and the simultaneous tribute from the greatest poet of the age. T. S. Eliot's article for the *T.L.S.* of 31 March 1921, reprinted in the volume of *Tercentenary Tributes* from Hull[2] appeared along with tributes from other distinguished elders that left Marvell a minor poet—a favourite line 'might have been culled from Mr Ralph Hodgson'. Into this cosy volume with its nostalgic pictures of Hull's decorated tram cars, T. S. Eliot M.A. (as he is described) propels Marvell as the companion rather of Catullus, part of the main European poetic tradition that includes Gautier, Baudelaire, and Laforgue. The tradition is defined in terms of 'Wit'. Understanding of Marvell's wit as identified by Eliot here and in his review of Grierson's anthology brought Marvell back to life—'the great, the perennial task of criticism' as Eliot believed. He became great, as he became our contemporary.

Wit, 'a tough reasonableness beneath the slight lyric grace', combines variety with order so that 'the wit forms the crescendo and diminuendo of a scale of great imaginative power'. An 'alliance of levity with seriousness by which the seriousness is intensified' had been revived by the French symbolists.

> Le squelette était invisible
> Au temps heureux de l'art paien!

links with 'To his Coy Mistress' Eliot, in *The Waste Land*, finished later in 1921, echoes Marvell's poem in his own witty transformation.

> But at my back from time to time I hear
> The sounds of horns and motors, which shall bring
> Sweeney to Mrs Porter in the spring.
> O the moon shone bright on Mrs Porter
> And on her daughter
> They wash their feet in soda water
> *Et O ces voix d'enfants chantant dans la coupole!*
> [196–202]

Marvell and the Elizabethan John Day are coupled with that bawdy song the Australian troops sang at Gallipoli—where Eliot's friend Jean Verdenal had been killed.[3] In the decade following the First World War, fragments of the collapsed civilization that supposedly was being saved were juxtaposed with absurdities of the present, enabling the poets to suggest a horror for which they had no words—the total breakdown of reason, sense, and order. Eliot defined Wit as 'probably a recognition, implicit in the expression of every experience, of other kinds of experience which are possible', recording his particular debt.

The quality which Marvell had, this modest and certainly impersonal virtue—whether we call it wit or reason or even urbanity ... is something precious and needed and apparently extinct.

In his companion essay on the Metaphysical Poets, Eliot declared that 'the poet's mind is constantly amalgamating disparate experience' but that in the seventeenth century poets 'possessed a mechanics of sensibility which could devour any kind of experience'. Attempting to write on the war, his friend Ezra Pound alternated wit with violence:

> There died a myriad
> And of the best, among them,
> For an old bitch gone in the teeth,
> For a botched civilization.
> [*Hugh Selwyn Mauberley*, 1920,v]

'Poetry must be difficult' was Eliot's conclusion; comparisons with Tennyson, Browning, and Morris distinguished between the intellectual and the reflective poet, and suggest the greater maturity of the metaphysical style.

Curiously enough, however, no one connected the new relevance of Marvell with the fact that he too had lived through a period of war that brought dramatic changes in the social thought and social practice of this country.

However, Eliot's essay altered the stature of Marvell more decisively than he could have ever expected. In my undergraduate days, during the late twenties, the edition of Margoliouth and the biography of Pierre Legouis supplied the scholarly equipment for a major poet. (It is a pity that the English version of Legouis cuts down his valuable biographical material in the interests of his rather eccentric critical views.) At Cambridge T. S. Eliot had delivered the Clark Lectures on Metaphysical Poetry; in his *Practical Criticism* I. A. Richards expounded 'To his Coy Mistress' which for these years was the poem of poems. The lines recalled by Eliot

> But at my back I alwaies hear
> Times winged Charriot hurrying near:
> And yonder all before us lye
> Desarts of vast Eternity

or the concluding couplet of that stanza

> The Grave's a fine and private place,
> But none I think do there embrace

as Eliot remarked and Richards developed, exemplified Coleridge's doctrine of the Imagination.

This power . . . reveals itself in the balance or reconciliation of opposite or discordant qualities; of sameness with difference, of the general with the concrete; the idea with the image; the individual with the representative, the sense of novelty and freshness with old and familiar objects; a more than usual state of judgement with more than usual order with enthusiasm and feeling profound and vehement. [*Biographia Literaria*, Chapter XIV]

This definition of the Theory of Imagination we applied to the poems of Marvell which we knew by heart, felt to be part of the texture of our daily living

I hope you will pardon my giving this personal and local testimony since these views spread from Cambridge to other places. In that period of the rapid growth of comparative studies (in anthropology, for instance) when 'an absence of all belief' could be attributed by Richards to *The Waste Land* as a virtue, Marvell provided the historical root for new poetry. The earnestness of the Victorians (with the exception of Hopkins, another discovery of the time), the enthusiasm of the Romantics seemed equally out of key, but the metaphysical poets were true ancestors; in Marvell their qualities were concentrated.

His approach, rather than the stresses behind it, love poetry and pastoral rather than the political verse, fulfilled these needs. E. M. Forster in the course of the first world war had praised Eliot for a similar detachment:

For what, in a world of horror was tolerable except the lighter gestures of dissent?.... he who could turn aside to complain of ladies and drawing rooms preserved a tiny drop of our self-respect, he carried on the human heritage. [*Abinger Harvest*, 1936, p. 88]

Leavis, who found in *Hugh Selwyn Mauberley* words for what he would never speak of directly—his own war experience—stressed Eliot's terms for Marvell of 'urbanity' and 'poise'. In *How to Teach Reading, a Primer for Ezra Pound* (1932) he opened his 'scheme of work' with the advice to read Eliot on Marvell and the metaphysical poets, and Grierson's preface to his anthology; Eliot's comparison of 'The Nymph Complaining for the Death of her Fawn' with Morris's 'Song to Hylas' became one of his favourite class exercises. In *Revaluation* (1936), Leavis compared Marvell with Herrick; in *Scrutiny* *XIII* (1945) comparing 'An Horatian Ode' with Lionel Johnson on the statue of King Charles at Charing Cross, he once more praised Marvell's 'urbanity' and 'poise':

It is in the nature of Marvell's ode not to be a product of strong personal emotion (there is no evidence in it that Marvell had any to control) but to be the poised formal expression of statesmanlike wisdom, surveying judicially the contemporary scene [p. 65].

William Empson first began to recognize the underlying emotion; he discussed Marvell's elegy for Lord Hastings in *Seven Types of Ambiguity* (1930) and 'The Garden' in *Some Versions of Pastoral* (1936). As you have already heard Empson, both a Yorkshireman and a poet, I should wish to say only that the political imagery in his own poetry is Marvellian. Such lines as

> Love makes long spokes of the short stakes of men,

or

> Fly with me then to all and the world's end
> And plumb for safety down the gulf of stars,

or

> You can't beat English lawns. Our final hope
> Is flat despair,

combine the techniques of wit with the perspectives of science; but in 'Flighting for Duck', set on the Ouse, the ominous shades of war and 'a drumming in the sky' suggest the technique that Marvell used for oblique political reference in 'Upon Appleton House'. There is a 'hint of anti-aircraft' and a galactic metaphor combined, but it all appears casual, the levity enforcing the seriousness. What finally emerges is a black mourning band round his hat.

> Starlit, mistcircled, one whole pearl embrowned
> An even silver dusk of earth and sky
> Held me dazzled with cobwebs, staring round,
> The black band of my hat leapt to my eye.
> Alone in sight not coloured like the ground
> It lit, like a struck match, everything by.

Nimble word games are played with exact details—the 'ground' is a burial earth on which the duck fall, the struck match ominous of war.

Interest in Marvell's wider *oeuvre*, and especially his historic commitments grew relevant in the darkening days of the later thirties. Gwyneth Lloyd Thomas and I wrote on him in the last number of Eliot's quarterly, *The Criterion* which appeared in

January 1939; and when in 1940, our little book came out, we felt the sustaining voice of one who had also known the dilemmas of war, and the shame and humiliation that we felt at the betrayal of Bohemia.

God direct all councils to the true remedy of the urgent condition of this poor nation, which I hope there is no reason to despair of,

he wrote in March 1677 to the burgesses of Hull.

If in the years of war, Marvell seemed in a new way our contemporary, the years of peace saw his complete conquest of American graduate schools. The New Critics, in their search for 'tension' and 'ambiguity', were led inevitably to Marvell. Cleanth Brooks's essay on the Horatian ode, appearing in 1947, opened with a general manifesto:[4]

A poem has a life of its own . . . . it provides in itself the only criterion by which it can be judged.

In the Ode, 'the attitude is not inhuman in its detachment' for 'though a monument of impartiality, it is not a monument of indifference'. As Eliot had found levity a reinforcement to seriousness, so Brooks thinks complexity springs from 'the kind of honesty and insight and wholemindedness that we associate with tragedy'—so that 'the admiration and condemnation do not cancel each other. They define each other and because there is responsible definition they reinforce each other'. Douglas Bush, retorting that Cleanth Brooks was turning a seventeenth-century liberal into a modern one by detecting irony in the praise of Cromwell, initiated a brisk controversy about the intention of this Ode, which with intervals has lasted from that day to this.

This has been for some years Marvell's most debated poem. One young English critic declared that the poise and urbanity, if they existed, were the poise and urbanity of a man upon the rack; secret readings that contradict the overt meaning have been detected, so that 'the forward youth that would appear' becomes the suicidal leader of a Royalist last stand—an extreme example of what have been termed double-edged meanings. So the Ode becomes something like the Jacobite toast:

> God bless the king—I mean the faith's defender
> God bless—no harm in blessing—the Pretender.

> Who that Pretender is, and who that king,
> God bless us all, is quite another thing.

This secret reading has even been extended to the love poems, which are read as political poems in disguise.[5]

The flatly opposing views are summarized by John Wallace in *Destiny his Choice* (1968). Cromwell has been termed the Scourge of God, the Dux Bellorum, the Davidic King. The hard process of decision is now read as a very costly thing. As Wallace puts it in defining 'loyalism' as the decision to work with a *de facto* ruler:

> Loyalism was created from chaos, in those moments of desperation when the only conceivable action is the performance of daily routine. [p. 41]

All moderate men, of whatever belief, were united in grief and shame at the execution of the King, yet

> the acquiescence of many godly ministers who had sworn to protect not only the king but his heirs should not be regarded as a lamentable exhibition of human weakness but a deeply religious response to the sadness of the times and the responsibilities of government. [pp. 42–3]

Nowadays, dilemmas of collaboration or dissidence, the knife-edge decisions imposed in revolutionary régimes, are but too familiar. The patient builder of bridges (in South Africa, for instance) who, disapproving of nearly every act of his government in certain directions, yet refers to 'my country' is not taken as a coward. Yet again Marvell has proved our contemporary; in a society open to violence, we recognize the value of an outward preservation of the façade of decency—'Assume a virtue if you have it not.'

The deep divisions of the Civil War appear in the poetry, according to a recent and brilliant suggestion of Christopher Ricks, in those self-reflective images that in Marvell represent one subject as *both* terms in a comparison; the drop of dew that shines 'like its own tear', the Body impaled by the Soul till 'mine own Precipice I go'. Isabel MacCaffrey sees in the imaginative wit of 'Upon Appleton House' a capacity to accept appalling facts, like massacre, by playing with them.[6]

By the strength of its alternative lines, the stanza form of the

'Horatian Ode' allows variety of stress—and it has meant different things to different generations in this century. It has been urged that the definition of a classic is just that—it must always 'signify more than is needed by any one interpreter or generation of interpreters'.[7] It becomes a fountain of new and valid interpretations, as it combines with and interacts upon the generations. Any self-indulgent demand that poetry should be 'relevant', if it means that we are not prepared to learn anything but only to enlarge our own prejudices and preconceptions, will not meet that flexibility which the reader in his turn must bring to his reading; Marvell of course asks a good deal of his readers. The history of Marvell our contemporary extends beyond his secular politics to ecclesiastical concerns in his later prose, where for instance that image of the precipice is put to very different use (*The Rehearsal Transpros'd*, ed. Smith, p. 30).

As American scholars of the history of ideas moved to rescue Marvell from the New Critics and the formidable phalanxes of Baltimore and Chicago advanced, the notion of wit disappeared under a load of learning. Rosemond Tuve took on T. S. Eliot with his 'direct translation of thought into feeling' with a study of traditional figures; Ruth Wallerstein sought the medieval and scholastic basis of metaphysical thought. No poem was more fully overhauled than 'The Nymph Complaining for the Death of her Fawn'. Gwyneth Lloyd Thomas and I had done no more than note the analogies with 'The Song of Songs' and the overtones associated by biblical gloss with that ancient love poem. This was hardened into systematic symbolism or even allegory; the debate pro and con again lasted for years and for all I know still continues. Since 1940 we have all learnt much about iconography and our views will be better informed; but the excessive piling up of classical, theological, rhetorical commentary produced its own reaction.

Frank Kermode, who in 1952 applied to Marvell's 'The Garden' the conventions of the Garden Poem as a special form or *genre*, was moved to enter a strong caveat.[8] He thinks those 'norms' which permit a theory of genres (and counter-genres) must not be hardened into a series of propositions: 'The necessity is to distinguish between the *genre* and the history of ideas, to which the *genre* is related.' Written in the language of the conventional Garden Poem, Marvell's 'Garden' actually refutes the traditional assumptions of this genre; it is the garden in the desert, the garden of the solitary, not the Garden of Delights.

Kermode's plea is directed against 'specially got-up learning' whereby 'To his Coy Mistress' becomes a statement refuting Hobbes, spiritualizing the Deism of Herbert of Cherbury, cementing something or other which the Cambridge Platonists thought they found in Descartes. For these observations Kermode awards the booby prize to a book entitled *Marvell's Ironic Vision*. Scholarship, says Kermode, needs humane justification, a sense of the civilized probabilities, and a habitually suspicious attitude to one's own scholarly self-regard. Unless this occurs 'the poet is in for a period of torture, one scholar pumping foreign matter into him as another sucks it out for regurgitation, rather like the cormorants in "The Unfortunate Lover"':

> And as one Corm'rant fed him, still
> Another on his Heart did bill,
> Thus while they famished him, and feast,
> He both consumed, and increast.

There is, however, a mitigating circumstance which neither Kermode, nor John Carey, who three years later followed him in baiting the Americans,[9] have allowed for.

That main European tradition (with which Eliot identified Marvell's poetry) is still directly accessible in certain favoured climates; but what can be breathed in at Oxford or Paris must be verbalized, even spelt out, in the American mid-west. Marvell's poems are the little door by which access to this great cultural tradition is gained; then, rather as archaeologists remake a whole civilization from fragments of a ruined city—laboriously and with drudgery—the critics reconstruct through Marvell a total recall of what lay not in, but behind the poems. Admittedly from the point of view of history this is totally to invert the premise of Cleanth Brooks, and make a poem into a cultural digest; from the literary point of view it is putting the cart before the horse. But it is a good way to focus an alien subject.

A second point is, in American academic convention it appears that any explanation which is at all tenable should be offered, to provide material for literary debate. Because debate is still the favoured mode of instruction, not the probable but the possible is expounded, and up to the limit. In 1970 no less than four books on Marvell appeared from the Americans; Ann Berthoff presented 'The Unfortunate Lover' as an allegory of the soul's life on earth, 'The Definition of Love' as the soul's longing for a Platonic heavenly self, the floral dial of 'The Garden' as not a floral dial but an analogue for the Garden itself. The other three all concentrated on the pastoral genre, but in no mood of ease or gaiety.[10]

The Americans were turning, as they tend to do in time of stress or war, to dreams of a happier, better world, to be gained by toil and virtue: to the American Dream. Marvell's pastoral became ever more lofty and Platonic, the more the old Frontier was seen to lie at the ports of embarcation for Vietnam. In the late 1960s the Americans were doing to Marvell what the English had done in 1921—they were playing E. M. Forster's gambit.

By 1970 the need was so urgent that pastoral and anti-pastoral were found everywhere; *King Lear*, save the mark, was thought to be enhanced by terming it anti-pastoral. Rosalie Colie, who furnished the extreme of this line, combined the stylistics of Rosemond Tuve, the medieval proclivities of Ruth Wallerstein with a scrupulous reading that produced footnotes with anything up to twenty citations each from the Marvell industry, including unpublished dissertations and forthcoming articles that had not yet seen the light of day. She was sensitively alive to the poetry, as any one who met her would learn; yet the effect of her book on me was a strong desire to find my way to that little chapel, nearly filled with the Fairfax tomb, sit there and read 'Little Gidding'.

By contrast, as I have indicated, the English Marvell of these years was an agonized figure, whose poetry of the Civil War was in theme the same as his satires of the Restoration. 'Upon Appleton House' has been prominent, and for all I know Marvell is about to be annexed by the English Revolutionaries, as Christopher Hill has already attached Milton to that particular Good Old Cause. If some readers see the 'Horatian Ode' as carrying an encoded message for royalists, others, like R. V. Hodges and M. D. Long, might be assuming that in the hour of our peril Cromwell will return and deal with all commentators as Colonel Pride and his followers dealt with the Long Parliament. And why should not these troops come from Cambridge, since there Cromwell's head reposes, secretly interred in his old College, the precise spot being known only to the Master and one other? Marvell might be investigated in a spirit of radicalism, till his earlier career was found to chime completely with his later one.[11]

The criticism of Marvell has now swollen to such proportions that, whilst in 1960 Lloyd Berry found it practicable to compile a bibliography of recent writing on metaphysical poetry, by 1975 Gillian Szanto needed more than a dozen pages to deal with 'Recent Studies in Marvell' and even then was three years in arrear.[12]

Perhaps some solution may be discerned in a recent study of rhetoric by Richard Lanham, *The Motives of Eloquence* (Yale, 1976). It is not directly concerned with Marvell but describes how formal education trained men to see their world in terms of *pro* and *con* (like a soldier studying and imitating his enemy). Rhetorical man, imaginative and dialectic, will inevitably conflict with the inner self, the Platonic self, who is committed to a scale of values; for rhetorical man can always see in every experience other kinds of experience that are possible, as Eliot predicated of Marvell. For example, George Chapman a firm Protestant, could put a case for the Massacre of St. Bartholomew. Rhetoric accustomed its students to a world of contingent purposes; it offered both a training in imaginative tolerance and weapons for battle. Compare in Marvell's prose the effects of the 'bantering' style in *The Rehearsal Transpros'd* with the more indirect way in which a supposedly impartial Reporter is allowed in *The Growth of Popery* to slant his material.[13]

Marvell's pleasure in inverting the rules of whatever game he was playing can be seen in his verses in comparisons of love and war. In 'Daphnis and Chloe' the hero had not digested the lesson provided by the Wooden Horse at Troy and

> Knew not that the Fort to gain
> Better 'twas the Siege to raise.

In 'The Fair Singer' and 'To his Coy Mistress' the 'rough strife' is more playful, but in 'The Definition of Love', energy liberated by renunciation appears yet more paradoxically. Why should Marvell not use the garden of love to repudiate social commitments, as he was to use a form of praise, in 'Last Instructions to a Painter', for satire? This is in itself a traditional gambit, one understood by such a practical man as Samuel Pepys, who was clearly very taken with this work, and even thought of doing something of the same kind himself.[14]

Marvell had been raised in this great parliamentary stronghold of Hull, where the action in-closing the city gates against the King marked the outbreak of the Civil War. Yet his own sympathies were at first Royalist; from the first he would have had to balance his beliefs. In later life as he told the burgesses 'I am naturally and now more by my age inclined to keep my thoughts private' (*Letters to Hull*, No 197). He did not even publish such a public poem as that on the victory obtained by Blake. Recently we have been given evidence that he acted as a secret agent for the Dutch underground (code name 'Mr. Thomas'); Mrs. Duncan-Jones thinks there is some reason to believe that Mary Palmer may have been justified in her claim to have married Marvell at a church noted for clandestine marriages, Holy Trinity in the Little Minories—a 'royal peculiar' like the Chapel at the Savoy.

An inner self, a Platonic self, a 'secret self of self, most strange, most still/Fast furled and all foredrawn to No or Yes' may be assumed from the strength and conviction of Marvell's rhythm, and also from the playfulness of his wit. For if wit is called forth by conflict, the ability to toy with an idea is itself a sign of adjustment. 'Negative capability' is needful for any who would be a builder of bridges; contraries are not negatives. The 'Horatian Ode' is no more detached and uncommitted[15] than the 'Last Instructions', where the murdered Charles reappears as a ghost. Or, if in any sense the poem is detached that is because it is committed, far too deeply committed to be partisan.

The most intricate and elaborate in structure of Marvell's lyrics are his religious pieces; I shall end with a look at 'The Coronet' as an illustration of the dialogue between the rhetorical and the committed self. This poem has not received too much attention; it is true that one commentator saw the 'fragrant towers that once adorned my Shepherdesses head' as 'the finery of a recherché bawd'. It has been seen as a case of pastoral and anti-pastoral, and an invitation to pile up biblical analogues. It has not been noted that the plainly direct conclusion, which resolves the poem's intricacies, changes the style from narrative to prayer; the poem is no longer meditative, but an address to a person, 'Thou'; the commitment is to an I–Thou relation, not to a principle. The intricate weavings of the rhetorical self produce a Coronet—a term itself so loaded with tragic implications for Marvell's generation that the unspoken memory of a royal crown vibrates against the pastoral crown of the shepherd and the Crown of Thorns. An acuter eye detects through the foliage not 'the hatching throstle's shining eye' but the inexpugnable enemy within.

> Thinking (so I myself deceive)
> So rich a Chaplet thence to weave
> As never yet the king of Glory wore:
> Alas I find the Serpent old
> That, twining with his speckled breast,
> About the flow'rs disguis'd does fold,
> With wreaths of Fame and Interest.

The transformation in rhythm and in address then comes with something of the break between octet and sestet in a sonnet:

> But thou who only couldst the Serpent tame,
> Either his slipp'ry knots at once untie,
> And disentangle all his winding Snare:
> Or shatter too with him my curious frame:
> And let these wither, so that he may die,
> Though set with Skill and chosen out with Care.

These hesitancies and reluctancies lead up to a clinching couplet which kinetically concludes the action with as it were two feet firmly planted together; alluding to the bruising of the serpent in Genesis 3.

> That they, whilst thou on both their Spoils dost tread,
> May crown thy Feet, that could not crown thy Head.

The pun in 'spoils', reinforcing the sense of difficulty in the conquest, may suggest secular icons of victors trampling on the vanquished. The deepest conquest lies in the surrender implied in the appeal 'But, Thou.' Marvell uses the intimate second person at the end of the 'Horatian Ode' to dissolve the rhetorical antithesis, by direct address to Cromwell. Again the work of the serpent as described in the address to England in 'Upon Appleton House', produces the intimate form of address.

> O Thou, that dear and happy Isle,
> The Garden of the World ere while, ...
> What luckless Apple did we taste,
> To make us Mortal, and Thee Waste? [321–8]

As a professional linguist and diplomat, Marvell's sense of address was delicate, his concern with what would now be termed 'the media' exceptionally wide. Had it not been controlled by incorruptible principle and inflexible resolve, prostitution of his talent would have been easy. The tension between his skill in manipulating points of view together with the niceties of public address and his authentic convictions, is a tension which for anyone living in the world of today has increased and is increasing. Here, yet again, he remains our contemporary.

NOTES

1. See H. J. C. Grierson, *Metaphysical Poetry from Donne to Butler* (Oxford 1921), p. xxxvii.
2. *Andrew Marvell 1621–1678*, ed. W. H. Bagguley (Oxford 1922), pp. 63–78.
3. Eliot's first volume of poems had been dedicated to Jean Verdenal.
4. Cleanth Brooks, 'Criticism and Literary History: Marvell's "Horatian Ode"', *Sewanee Review*, 55 (1947), pp. 199–222.
5. See J. M. Newton, *The Cambridge Quarterly*, VI, I (1973), pp. 125–42. By contrast see A. J. N. Wilson, *The Critical Quarterly*, 11, 4 (Winter 1969), pp. 325–43. Part of the difficulty lies in the overt royalism of 'Tom May's Death' as May died 13 November, 1650. It is probably part of some literary game to which 'The Great Assises' also belonged; their satire is literary, not political.
6. See her article in *Tercentenary Essays in Honor of Andrew Marvell*, ed. K. Friedenreich (Archon Books, Hamden, Connecticut, 1977), pp. 224–44. Christopher Ricks's article will appear in *Aspects of Marvell*, ed. C. A. Patrides (Routledge, Kegan Paul, 1978).
7. Frank Kermode, *The Classic* (1975), p. 140.
8. Frank Kermode 'The Argument of Marvell's "Garden"', *Essays in Criticism*, II (1952), pp. 225–41; 'Marvell Transpros'd', *Encounter* (November 1966), pp. 77–84.

9. John Carey (ed.), *Andrew Marvell*, Penguin Critical Anthologies (1969), pp. 61–71.
10. Ann Berthoff, *The Resolved Soul* (Princeton U.P., 1970); Rosalie Colie, *My Ecchoing Song* (Princeton U.P., 1969); Patrick Cullen, *Spenser, Marvell and Renaissance Pastoral* (Harvard U.P., 1970); Donald Friedman, *Marvell's Pastoral Art* (California U.P., 1970).
11. This would of course be in complete contrast to the views mentioned in note 5.
12. Gillian Szanto, 'Recent Studies in Marvell', *English Literary Renaissance*, 5 (1975), pp. 273–86.
13. See Annabel Patterson 'Naked or Otherwise: Marvell's Account of the Growth of Popery and Arbitrary Government', *Studies in the Literary Imagination*, X, 2 (1977), pp. 115–28 (Atlanta, Georgia); and compare Isabel MacCaffrey, *Modern Philology*, 61 (1964), pp. 261–9.
14. See Samuel Pepys: *Diary*, ed. R. W. Latham (G. Bell, 1971–4), VI, p. 207; VII, p. 407; VIII, pp. 21 and 439. (I am indebted to Mr. Latham for these references.)
15. The collocation is J. B. Leishman's.
16. The 'curious frame' is both literary and physical, of course; see Chapman's use of this term in *Ovid's Banquet of Sense* (1595), stanze 117. Here it means both a sequence of events and the artistic disposition of that sequence, its interpretation.

POSTSCRIPT

A Commemorative Address given by the Lord President of the Council, the Rt. Hon. Michael Foot, M.P., at the Civic Luncheon in the Guildhall, Hull, on 10 February 1978.

I wish to offer my congratulations to the city of Hull for the manner in which they are celebrating Andrew Marvell. He was certainly not an orthodox figure, and it is all the more commendable, therefore, that he should have proper recognition paid to him.

He was a poet of great delicacy, and also of some indelicacy. He was a Parliamentarian but he was also a revolutionary. And indeed, during most of the twenty years when he represented this city in the House of Commons, he was swimming against the tide and at loggerheads with the authorities.

Only a few months before his death—that is just about exactly 300 years ago—he had what I think might have been described as an altercation in the corridors of the House of Commons and was nearly sent to the Tower by officious apologists to the monarch and the government of the time. I am glad to see that none of those memories has dissuaded the city from doing him proper honour. But then, of course, the city of Hull—second only perhaps to the city of Plymouth, my native city—had a splendid record of service to Parliament throughout the whole epoch of the great Civil War and the Commonwealth, and it is good to see that that fine old allegiance retains its vitality today.

Parliament has played a central part in the history of England as is the case in that of no other country. It was the English people (with the aid of some occasional Celtic guides), who first set out on that course of democratic revolution without any maps to assist them. And during that period, contrary to many subsequent distortions, our people reached a stature which dwarfed their normal selves. That spirit was most wonderfully expressed in the prose and poetry of John Milton. And then—to quote H. N. Brailsford—'When Secretary Milton's eyes could see his pen no longer, there was an Andrew Marvell to pick it up.'

Yet it must be swiftly added that, for all his debt to Milton, Andrew Marvell was an originator himself—in the few most memorable poems which we read in all the anthologies, and, more still perhaps, in the style of prose writing which he fashioned to conduct his political battles. The very first student to note the fibre and strength of Marvell's prose, and the greatest, was Jonathan Swift. Mostly those pieces are unread today since they deal with inscrutable controversies of a bygone age. But there is no doubt about the force and the clarity of his English, all of which Swift discerned and over the years enfolded in his own style.

Indeed, as Christopher Hill has taught us to appreciate, the manner in which the English language itself was used was altered during the Commonwealth years, and no one played a more significant part in that alteration than Andrew Marvell himself. During those tempestuous years, the way the English people talked to one another acquired a fresh Ironside sinew to add to the Elizabethan richness.

'We are English, that is one good fact', is how Oliver Cromwell himself put it in what, I suppose, is the simplest and perhaps the best patriotic English speech ever uttered. Andrew Marvell spoke that same language and embraced it in his famous Horatian Ode. Incidentally, the best known line in that ode refers magnanimously to Charles I and his demeanour in that historic scene. But the hero, let no one doubt, was Cromwell. 'So much one man can do that does both act and know.'

It is an astonishing and sobering thought to remember that most of the poems which our children, I hope, are now taught in school—for example, the most famous one of all, 'To his Coy Mistress', or 'The Nymph Complaining for the Death of her Faun', 'Daphnis and Chloe', 'The Definition of Love', and so many others—were, like furious political satires, not published at all or published only anonymously in his lifetime. That makes it all the more necessary and creditable that he should be properly commemorated now.

He was pre-eminently the poet of Cromwell and of the Protectorate, and all through almost the whole period when he served this city so well he was, in the House of Commons and in the anonymous satires he was writing at the time, a kind of one-man opposition. Since the Government of that time was the worst in all our records—with perhaps a few modern exceptions, such as the one which led us into the Second World War—it was a most creditable role for a man to play. He was convinced that nothing would go right for us whilst the Stuarts remained on the throne. Most of us can accept that doctrine today, but it was not so easy to hold to the truth so firmly when Stuart despotism and Stuart pillories and Stuart thumbscrews were so near at hand.

I said that the English people learnt to talk a new language during that period, and that Andrew Marvell was one of the foremost instructors. As I turned over those pages in preparation for coming here today, I read a few sentences from Oliver Cromwell which Andrew Marvell himself might have penned. I felt them to be so apposite to our present occasion that I would like to leave them with you as the final thought.

How to make good our station, to improve the mercies and successes God has given us, and not to be fooled out of them again, not to be broken in pieces by our particular jarrings and animosities one against another, but to unite our counsels.

Good advice, believe me, in this year 1978, if we are to sustain the great democratic tradition which the city of Hull and Andrew Marvell upheld together in language which all the forces of reaction and censorship will never be able to mangle or suppress.

INDEX

Abinger Harvest, 107
Account of the Growth of Popery . . . in England, An, 26, 114, 118
Adams, J. Q., 103
Adwalton Moor, 9
Agrippa, Henry Cornelius, 43, 45
Albemarle, Duke of, *see* Monck, George
All For Love, 51
'Ancient Mariner, The Rime of the', 55
Andrew Marvell (Penguin Critical Anthologies), 61, 118
Andrew Marvell, Poet, Puritan, Patriot, 32, 47, 61, 106
Andrew Marvell: Some Biographical Background, 33
Andrew Marvell, Tercentenary Essays in Honor of, 117
Andrew Marvell Tercentenary Exhibition: Descriptive Catalogue, 32
Andrew Marvell: Tercentenary Tributes, 35, 104, 117
Andrew Marvell: the Complete Poems, 32
Appleton, *see* Nunappleton
Aristotle, 45
Arlington, Henry Bennet, Earl of, 21
Aspects of Marvell, 117
Aubrey, John, 1, 3, 27, 32, 35, 69, 92, 94, 95, 103

Bagguley, W. H., 35, 117
Baudelaire, Charles, 104
Bellasis, John, Lord, 19
'Bermudas', 67, 99–102
Berry, Lloyd, 114
Berthoff, Ann, 113, 118
Beverley, 3
Biographia Literaria, 106–7
Birrell, Augustine, 31
Blake, Robert, 115
Blaydes, James, 6, 37
Bordeaux, 20, 38
Boston, Mass., 31
Brailsford, H. N., 119
Bradshaw, John, 9, 12, 38
Brooks, Cleanth, 72, 109, 112, 117
Browne, Sir Thomas, 92
Browning, A., 35

Browning, Robert, 106
Buckingham, George Villiers, Duke of, 9, 35, 58
Burdon, Pauline, 33
Burke, Edmund, 24
Burnet, Bishop Gilbert, 23, 34, 68
Burney, James, 3
Bush, Douglas, 72, 109
Butler, Samuel, 75

Cambridge, 1, 2, 3, 4, 5, 6, 37, 40, 106, 114
Capel, Sir Henry, 26
Carey, John, 36, 61, 112, 118
Carlisle, Charles Howard, Earl of, 19
Castlemaine, Barbara Palmer, Countess of, 21
Catullus, 104
Chapman, George, 114, 118
'Character of a Trimmer, The', 22
'Character of Holland, The', 12, 16, 33
Charles I, 5, 8, 9, 10, 12, 13, 14, 18, 22, 24, 56, 59, 74–86, 88, 89, 90, 92, 107, 115, 120
Charles II, 16, 18, 21, 22, 23, 24, 25, 26, 27, 29, 51, 56, 57, 58, 62, 69, 82, 89, 90, 96
Chatham, 21
Clarendon, Edward Hyde, Earl of, 21, 53, 54, 55, 57, 68, 74, 86, 87, 88
'Clarendon's House-Warming', 53, 56, 58
Cleveland, John, 88
Coleridge, S. T., 36, 76, 106
Colie, Rosalie, 113, 118
Commonwealth and Restoration Stage, The, 103
Cooke, Thomas, 23, 29, 30
Coolidge, J. S., 102
'Coronet, The', 40, 59, 115–16
Cowley, Abraham, 85
Criterion, The, 108
Cromwell, Elizabeth (Lady Claypole), 17
Cromwell, Mary (Lady Fauconberg), 17
Cromwell, Oliver, 5, 9, 10, 11, 12, 13, 14, 15, 16, 17, 18, 22, 24, 30, 33,

Cromwell, Oliver—*cont.*
    38, 59, 62, 63, 72, 73–86, 88, 89,
    91, 92, 109, 110, 113, 114, 117,
    120, 121
Cromwell: Our Chief of Men, 34
Cromwell, Richard, 17
Cruttwell, Patrick, 102
Cullen, Patrick, 118

'Damon the Mower', 48
Danby, Thomas Osborne, Earl of, 23,
    25, 27, 35, 58
'Daphnis and Chloe', 114, 120
Davies, Sir John, 10
Day, John, 105
Defensio Secunda, 13
'Definition of Love, The', 70, 113, 114,
    120
Defoe, Daniel, 92
Denham, Sir John, 10, 20, 75
Denmark, 19
De Occulta Philosophia, 45
Descartes, René, 112
Destiny His Choice, 33, 110
Dialogue between the Two Horses, A, 30,
    59
Diary of John Milward, The, 34
Discourse of Ecclesiastical Politie, A, 22
Donne, John, 65, 68, 104
Donno, Elizabeth Story, 32, 34
Dryden, John, 10, 17, 18, 30, 35, 39,
    51, 68, 69, 73, 80, 86, 104
Duncan-Jones, E. E., 32, 61, 102, 115
Dutton, William, 12, 16

Eikon Basilike, 89
Eikonoklastes, 12
'Elegy upon the Death of My Lord
    Francis Villiers, An', 9
Eliot, T. S., 31, 32, 79, 104, 105, 106,
    107, 108, 109, 111, 112, 117
Empson, Wm., 108
English Travellers Abroad 1604–1667, 32
'Epigramma in Duos Montes
    Amosclivum et Bilboreum:
    Farfacio', 11
Eton, 12, 16
Evans, Joan, 102

Fairfax, Lady, *née* Anne Vere, 10, 44,
    89
Fairfax, Mary, 11, 38, 47, 58, 71
Fairfax, Thomas, Lord, 8, 10, 11, 12,
    13, 14, 38, 39, 40, 43, 48, 71, 93,
    94
Fairfax, Sir Thomas, 8, 9
'Fair Singer, The', 114
Fanshawe, Sir Richard, 77
Farrington, John, 52
Ferens, T. R., 31
Fiennes, Celia, 92
'First Anniversary of the Government
    under O.C., The', 13, 14, 16,
    30, 33, 63, 72, 73, 91, 92, 94,
    101
Firth, Sir Chas., 32
'Flecknoe, an English Priest at Rome',
    28
Foix de Candale, François de, 40
Forster, E. M., 107, 113
Fraenkel, E., 102
France, 9
Fraser, Antonia, 34
Freud, Sigmund, 49
Friedenreich, K., 117
Friedman, D., 118

'Gallery, The', 97
'Garden, The', 40–6, 70, 99, 108, 111,
    113
Garroway, Joseph, 26
Gautier, Théophile, 104
Gerrard, Charles, Lord Gerrard and
    Earl of Macclesfield, 57
Gilby, Anthony, 19, 20
Golden Treasury, The, 104
Grey, Anchitel, 20, 34, 35
Grierson, Sir Herbert, 104, 117
Grosart, A. B., 32, 33, 35
Gwyn, Nell, 51

Hales, John, 12
Haley, K. H. D., 35, 58
Halifax, George Savile, Marquess of,
    22, 24
Harley, Sir Edward, 26
Harrington, John, 16, 26, 27
Hastings, Henry, Lord, 9
Hastings, Lady, *née* Lucy Davies, 10
Heirs of Donne and Jonson, The, 102
Henson, Bishop H. Hensley, 31
Henry IV, of France, 22
Herbert of Cherbury, Edward, Lord,
    112
Hermes Trismegistus, 40, 43
Herrick, Robert, 10, 64, 68, 69, 93, 107

Hessle, 4

Hill, Christopher, 33, 34, 113, 120

History and Description of Hull, A, 32

History of My Own Times, A, 34

History of the Rebellion, 53, 86, 87, 88

History of the Society of Antiquaries, A, 102

Hobbes, Thomas, 86, 91, 112

Hodges, R. V., 113

Hodgson, Ralph, 104

Holland, 9, 19

Hopkins, G. M., 107

Horace, 78, 79, 80, 82

'Horatian Ode upon Cromwell's Return from Ireland, An', 11, 13, 14, 68, 71–86, 88, 91, 92, 93, 102, 107, 109, 111, 113, 115, 117, 120

'Hortus', 44

Hotham, Sir John, 8, 9

Hotham, Captain John, 9

Hotson, Leslie, 103

Howard, Sir Robert, 26

How to Teach Reading: A Primer for Ezra Pound, 107

Hugh Selwyn Mauberley, 107

Hull, 1, 2, 3, 5, 6, 8, 9, 10, 11, 17, 18, 19, 23, 27, 29, 30, 31, 32, 36, 37, 38, 39, 49, 51, 52, 62, 96, 104, 108, 115, 119, 120, 121

Hyde, Edward, *see* Clarendon

Iliad, 54

Ingelo, Nathaniel, 3

Ireland, 11

Ireton, Henry, 10

Italy, 9

James II, 22

Jermyn, Henry, Earl of St. Albans, 20, 21

Johnson, Lionel, 107

Jonson, Ben, 65, 72, 75

Kermode, Frank, 45, 111, 112, 117

King Lear, 113

'Kings Vowes, The', 56, 58

Knights, L. C., 102

Korn, A. L., 102

Lachrymae Musarum, 10

Laforgue, Jules, 104

Lambert, Malet, 31

'Last Instructions to a Painter, The', 20, 21, 22, 23, 30, 63, 69, 82, 90, 115

Lanham, Richard, 114

Latham, R. W., 118

Laud, Archbishop, 4

Lawson, John, 3, 32

Leavis, F. R., 107–8

Leishman, J. B., 45, 118

Legouis, Pierre, 32, 33, 34, 35, 42, 43, 45, 46, 53, 55, 60, 61, 67, 72, 106

'Letter to Dr. Ingelo. . . . A', 3

Leviathan, 86

Long, M. D., 113

Lord, George de Forest, 34

Louis XIV, of France, 25, 26

Lovelace, Richard, 9, 13, 39, 68, 93

'Lovall Scot, The', 59

Lucasta, 9

MacCaffrey, Isabel, 110, 118

Machiavelli, Niccolo, 15

Machiavellian Moment, The, 33

Mallarmé, Etienne, 67

Margoliouth, H. M., 10, 32, 33, 34, 35, 56, 57, 58, 59, 61, 106

Marvell, Andrew:

 Life

  1–12, 16–29, 37–40, 49–52

 Works

  Account of the Growth of Popery, An, 26, 114, 118

  'Bermudas', 67, 99–102

  'Character of Holland, The, 12, 16, 33

  'Clarendon's House-Warming', 53, 56, 58

  'Coronet, The', 40, 59, 115–16

  'Damon the Mower', 48

  'Daphnis and Chloe', 114, 120

  'Definition of Love, The', 70, 113, 114, 120

  'Dialogue between the Two Horses, A', 30, 59

  'Elegy upon the Death of My Lord Francis Villiers, An', 9

  'Epigramma in Duos Montes Amosclivum et Bilboreum: Farfacio', 11

  'Fair Singer, The', 114

  'First Anniversary of the Government under O.C., The', 13, 14, 16, 30, 33, 63, 72, 73, 91, 92, 94, 101

Marvell, Andrew (*Works*)—*cont.*
  'Flecknoe, an English Priest at
    Rome', 28
  'Gallery, The', 97
  'Garden, The', 40–6, 70, 99, 108,
    111, 113
  'Horatian Ode upon Cromwell's
    Return from Ireland, An', 11,
    13, 14, 68, 71–86, 88, 91, 92, 93,
    102, 107, 109, 111, 113, 115,
    117, 120
  'King's Vowes, The', 56, 58
  'Last Instructions to a Painter,
    The', 20, 21, 22, 23, 30, 63, 69,
    82, 90, 115
  'Letter to Dr. Ingelo, A', 3
  'Loyall Scot, The', 59
  'Mower against Gardens, The', 67
  'Mower to the Glo-Worms, The', 98
  'Nymph Complaining for the Death
    of her Faun, The', 70, 96, 99,
    107, 120
  ['On Blood's Stealing the Crown'],
    30
  'On General Councils', 5, 32
  'On Mr. Milton's Paradise Lost',
    27, 30
  'Picture of Little T.C. in a Prospect
    of Flowers, The', 70
  'Poem upon the Death of O.C., A',
    13, 17, 32, 63, 72, 73
  Rehearsal Transpros'd, The, 22, 23,
    25, 30, 32, 33, 34, 35, 50, 61, 65,
    81, 89, 111, 114
  'Statue at Charing Cross, The', 53,
    56, 60
  'Statue in Stocks-Market, The', 56
  'To His Coy Mistress', 11, 59, 62,
    68, 70, 105, 106, 112, 114, 120
  'Tom May's Death', 39, 65, 71, 117
  'Unfortunate Lover, The', 97, 113
  'Upon Appleton House', 3, 11, 40,
    42, 44, 45, 46, 48, 58, 67, 69, 83,
    93, 98, 108, 110, 113, 117
  'Upon the Death of the Lord
    Hastings', 9, 108
  'Upon the Hill and Grove at
    Bilbrough', 11, 43
Marvell, the Rev. Andrew, 2, 4, 5, 6, 39
Marvell, Mrs. Andrew, *née* Anne Pease,
  2
Marvell, Mrs. Andrew, *née* Lucy
  Alured, 6, 7, 8

Marvell, Anne (Mrs. James Blaydes), 6
Marvell, Elizabeth (Mrs. Robert More),
  2, 7
Marvell, John, 2
Marvell, Mary (Mrs. Edmund Popple),
  2
Marvell, Mary, *see* Palmer, Mary
Marvell's Ironic Vision, 112
Marvell's Pastoral Art, 118
May, Thomas, 39
Mazzeo, J. A., 33
Meldreth, 2, 7
Meres, Sir Thomas, 26
*Metaphysical Poetry from Donne to
  Butler*, 117
Midsummer Night's Dream, A, 43
Milton, John, 4, 9, 12, 13, 15, 16, 17,
  18, 26, 27, 33, 68, 86, 88, 98,
  103, 113, 119, 120
Milton and the English Revolution, 34
Milward, John, 20, 34
Monck, George, 18, 20
Monmouth, James Scott, Duke of, 19,
  57
Morris, Wm., 106, 107
Motives of Eloquence, The, 114
'Mower against Gardens, The', 67
'Mower to the Glo-Worms, The', 98
'My Ecchoing Song', 118

Neile, Archbishop Richard, 4
Nelthorpe, Edward, 28
Nettleton, Robert, 29
Newcastle, William Cavendish, Duke
  of, 9
Newton, J. M., 117
Nunappleton, 8, 9, 11, 39, 40, 71
'Nymph Complaining for the Death of
  her Faun, The', 70, 96, 99, 107,
  120

Oceana, 16
'On Blood's Stealing the Crown', 30
'On General Councils', 5, 32
'On Mr. Milton's Paradise Lost', 27, 30
Owen, John, 16
Oxenbridge, John, 12, 99
Oxford, 88, 99, 112
Oxford Book of English Verse, The, 104

Palgrave, F. T., 104
Palmer, Mrs. Mary, 27, 28, 29, 35, 49,
  50, 51, 61, 115

Paradise Lost, 27, 86, 98
Parfitt, G. J. A., 33
Paris, 112
Parker, Samuel, 22, 23, 50, 51, 61
Patrides, C. A., 117
Patterson, Annabel, 118
Pease, George, 2
Pepys, Samuel, 23, 115, 118
Perrott, Richard, 4
Pett, Peter, 21
'Picture of Little T.C. in a Prospect of Flowers, The', 70
Pocock, J. G. A., 33
'Poem upon the Death of O.C., A', 13, 17, 32, 63, 72, 73
Poems and Letters of Andrew Marvell, The, 32, 61
Pomponazzi, Pietro, 44
Pope, Alexander, 69
Popple, Edmund, 6, 17, 37, 38
Popple, William, 6, 20, 34
Pound, Ezra, 105
Practical Criticism, 106
Pride, Colonel Thomas, 95, 114
Public Voices, 102
Puritanism and Revolution, 33
Pym, John, 24

Quiller-Couch, Sir Arthur, 104

Raleigh, Sir Walter, 65
Ramsden, John, 18
Ready and Easy Way to Establish a Free Commonwealth, A, 17
Rehearsal Transpros'd, The, 22, 23, 25, 30, 32, 33, 34, 35, 50, 61, 65, 81, 89, 111, 114
Religio Laici, 30
Renaissance and Seventeenth-Century Studies, 33
Resolved Soul, The, 118
Revaluation, 107
Richards, I. A., 106, 107
Ricks, Christopher, 110, 117
Robbins, Caroline, 34
Rome, 9
Royston, 2
Russia, 19

St. John, Oliver, 12
Saumur, 12, 16
Scotland, 5, 11, 18, 94
Scrutiny, 107

Seventeenth-Century English Literature, 102
Seven Types of Ambiguity, 108
Seymour, Sir Edward, 26
Sharp, John, 29
Shakespeare, Wm., 51, 65, 90
Shakespearean Playhouses, 103
Shakespearian Moment, The, 102
Sheehan, J. H., 32, 35
Silver Poets of the Seventeenth Century, 33
Simeone, Wm., 102
Sir John Berkenhead, 103
Skinner, Edward, 10
Skinner, Mrs. William, *née* Bridget Coke, 7, 10
Smith, D. I. B., 32, 33, 61
Some Versions of Pastoral, 108
Spain, 9, 10
Spenser, Marvell and Renaissance Pastoral, 118
'Statue at Charing Cross, The', 53, 56, 60
'Statue in Stocks-Market, The', 56
Stevenson, Anthony, 3
Stockholm, 3
Stoye, John, 32, 33
Styles, William, 5
Strong, Roy, 102
Summers, Joseph H., 102
Sweden, 19
Swift, Jonathan, 120
Szanto, Gillian, 114, 118

Tennyson, Alfred, Lord, 104, 106
Tenure of Kings and Magistrates, The, 12
Thomas, Gwyneth Lloyd, 108, 111
Thomas, P. W., 103
Thompson, Edward, 28, 30
Thompson, Sir Henry, 51, 52
Thompson, Richard, 28
'To His Coy Mistress', 11, 59, 62, 68, 70, 105, 106, 112, 114, 120
'Tom May's Death', 39, 65, 71, 117
Town Grammar School through Six Centuries, A, 32
Trinity College, Cambridge, 3, 6
Tupper, F. S., 35, 49, 61
Tuve, Rosemond, 111, 113

'Unfortunate Lover, The', 97, 113
'Upon Appleton House', 3, 11, 40, 42, 44, 45, 46, 48, 58, 67, 69, 83, 93, 98, 108, 110, 113, 117

'Upon the Death of the Lord Hastings', 9, 108
'Upon the Hill and Grove at Bilbrough', 11, 43
Urn Burial, 92

Van Dyck, Sir Anthony, 89, 102
Verdenal, Jean, 105, 117
Vermeer, Jan, 36
Verney, Sir Edmund, 88, 89
Villiers, Francis, Lord, 9
Virgil (Publius Vergilius Maro), 49

Wall, L. N., 35
Wallace, John M., 33, 35, 110
Waller, Edmund, 13, 17, 18, 20, 33, 75, 99, 101
Waller, Sir William, 87, 88, 90
Wallerstein, Ruth, 111, 113

Walpole, Sir Robert, 24
Warwick, Sir Philip, 18, 26
Waste Land, The, 105, 107
Wedgwood, C. V., 102
Whitelocke, Bulstrode, 3
William III, 25, 58
William of Orange and the English Opposition 1672–4, 35, 58
Williamson, Sir Joseph, 35
Wilson, A. J. N., 117
Winestead, 2
Wordsworth, William, 30
Wright, Edward, 36

York, 4, 5, 8, 28, 51, 52
York, Duchess of, *née* Anne Hyde, 20, 21
York, James, Duke of, 20, 21, 25, 27, 58
Young, Peter, 102